WHAT THE
BIBLE
SAYS

RANDY L. HENNE

WESTBOW
P R E S S®
A DIVISION OF THOMAS NELSON
& ZONDERVAN

WestBow Press books may be ordered through booksellers or by contacting:

WestBow Press
A Division of Thomas Nelson & Zondervan
1663 Liberty Drive
Bloomington, IN 47403
www.westbowpress.com
844-714-3454

Because of the dynamic nature of the Internet, any web addresses or
links contained in this book may have changed since publication and
may no longer be valid. The views expressed in this work are solely those
of the author and do not necessarily reflect the views of the publisher,
and the publisher hereby disclaims any responsibility for them.

Any people depicted in stock imagery provided by Getty Images are
models, and such images are being used for illustrative purposes only.
Certain stock imagery © Getty Images.

ISBN: 978-1-6642-1105-6 (sc)
ISBN: 978-1-6642-1106-3 (e)

Library of Congress Control Number: 2020922192

Print information available on the last page.

WestBow Press rev. date: 11/10/2020

CONTENTS

PREFACE

To begin, I would like to briefly explain my motivation for writing this book. I am not writing for money or recognition. I am not seeking praise for my knowledge of the Bible or for my skills at writing (such as they are). I have never published anything before, other than some technical papers and computer magazine articles. In fact, I didn't initially start writing this book with the intent of publishing it at all. I had simply planned to give a few copies to friends and family. Upon reading my initial drafts, though, some of my reviewers felt that my work would be of value to a wider audience, so here we are! If my words help even one person, it will have been worth the effort.

I do not claim to be an expert on the Bible. In the Acknowledgments, I'll point you to some people who know a lot more than I do, to whom you can turn for more information.

I have been a student of the Bible for many years, but I recently went through an experience that caused me to reevaluate everything I thought I knew. I gained a new appreciation for the Bible, approached it with much more focus and determination than before, and learned a lot. In the Afterword, I'll share some of my personal story.

As I have gotten older and encountered some health problems, I have gained a heightened awareness that I'm much closer to the end of my life on this earth than to the beginning. The COVID-19 pandemic, ongoing as I write this, has further increased my awareness of my mortality.

I'm not planning to depart anytime soon, but that timing is in God's hands, not mine. I do want to share what I've learned, hopefully in a very clear and simple way, in order to leave behind a meaningful legacy.

I am hopeful that some will read this because they know me and respect me, whether or not they're initially interested. Of course, I also hope that many who have never heard of me will read it as well!

Most of all, I am writing this with the hope that my loved ones, family, friends, and anyone else who may read this will become more interested in what the Bible says, will begin to study the Bible for themselves, and will come to know the One Whom the Bible is all about!

INTRODUCTION

The Bible, also known as the Holy Scriptures, is the best-selling book of all time. It has been translated into more languages than any other book. There is probably one in your home. If not, there was almost certainly one in the home where you grew up. If you're in a hotel room right now, there is likely one in the desk or nightstand. You can even download free copies through the Internet onto your computer, phone, or tablet.

However, the Bible often sits on the coffee table or on a shelf like an ornament or a good-luck charm. In reality, it has no value at all unless you read it!

You may have grown up going to Sunday school and learning many of the great stories of the Bible: Adam and Eve in the garden of Eden; Noah and the Flood; the Tower of Babel; Abraham and Isaac; Joseph and his brothers; Moses delivering the Hebrew slaves from Egypt; Joshua and the battle of Jericho; young David killing the giant Goliath; Daniel in the lion's den; and of course the life, death, and resurrection of Jesus. But there is so much more!

In fact, taking short excerpts from the Bible, such as those Sunday school lessons often did, can mislead us, or at least cause us to miss important topics such as the problem of man's sin, our need for salvation, and God's way of providing it. Also, the Bible contains the stories of many human beings, and all humans fail and make mistakes. We can't say, "Well, the Bible says so-and-so did such-and-such, so it must be okay!"

I'm mostly trying to limit my personal opinions and present only what the Bible itself says. I will be quoting hundreds of Bible verses from several different translations. I will actually be doing what I just warned against: giving you short excerpts from the Bible to illustrate my points. Please know that I am making a concerted effort to accurately express important biblical truths, and I am not trying to mislead or deceive you. However, I want to clearly state that the Bible needs to be taken in its entirety, not just in bits and pieces. The Bible itself says:

> _Everything_ in the Scriptures is God's Word. _All_ of
> it is useful for teaching and helping people and for
> correcting them and showing them how to live. (2
> Timothy 3:16 CEV)[1]

My purpose in writing this book is to spark your interest in studying the Bible on your own. If I raise some questions in your mind, or if you read some things you didn't know were in the Bible, don't just take my word for it! Reading books about the Bible is good, but reading the Bible itself is so much better!

I strongly encourage you to read the Bible for yourself!

---

[1] I have chosen to italicize as well as indent my Bible quotations to clearly set them apart from my own words. Any underlining in the quotations is mine, for added emphasis. I have occasionally added comments for clarity (shown in brackets and not italicized), and have sometimes omitted words for brevity (as indicated by ellipses).

1

WHY SHOULD WE CARE
ABOUT THE BIBLE?

I am not going to argue the existence of God. The beauty, splendor, and complexity of His creation—whether seen in the galaxies in the heavens, a beautiful sunset, or a newborn baby—present the only arguments necessary. It takes more faith to believe that all this happened spontaneously than to believe that an intelligent and all-powerful God created it. As the Bible says:

> *The heavens declare the glory of God; the skies proclaim the work of his hands. Day after day they pour forth speech; night after night they display knowledge.* (Psalms 19:1–2 NIV)

> *They [people] know the truth about God because he has made it obvious to them. For ever since the world was created, people have seen the earth and sky. Through everything God made, they can clearly see his invisible qualities—his eternal power and divine nature. So they have no excuse for not knowing God.* (Romans 1:19–20 NLT)

Only fools say in their hearts, "There is no God."
(Psalms 14:1 NLT)

What happens to anything left outside in the elements for a while? It deteriorates. The natural progression in this world is from complex to simple, from organized to disorganized, from beauty to decay, from birth to death. So how could random, unguided processes produce a human being, or for that matter even a one-celled amoeba?

The point I want to emphasize is this: if there *is* a God Who created this universe, then He and only He has the right to establish the rules and principles by which His universe operates.

If He does have such rules and principles, and if He expects us, his created beings, to fulfill some purpose in His universe, then it would be unfair if He did not clearly communicate those rules and principles to us. Fortunately, that is exactly what He has done. He has given us the Bible! You can think of the Bible as God's instruction manual for life.

The Bible is not just a book of ancient stories—it has real meaning and purpose for us today. In its own words:

Such things were written in the Scriptures long ago to teach us. And the Scriptures give us hope and encouragement as we wait patiently for God's promises to be fulfilled. (Romans 15:4 NLT)

Your word is a lamp to guide my feet, and a light for my path. (Psalms 119:105 NLT)

The Bible has a life of its own, and it has the power to change lives:

> *For the word of God is living and active, sharper than any two-edged sword, piercing to the division of soul and of spirit, of joints and of marrow, and discerning the thoughts and intentions of the heart.* (Hebrews 4:12 ESV)

As we shall see later, its most important purpose is to lead us to faith in Jesus Christ:

> *So then faith cometh by hearing, and hearing by the word of God.* (Romans 10:17 KJV)

WHAT DO WE KNOW
ABOUT THE BIBLE?

The Bible is actually not a single book but a collection of sixty-six books, written by many different authors over several thousand years. Despite this, the Bible itself claims that these authors were guided by the Spirit of God and wrote exactly what He wanted them to write! As it says:

> *All Scripture is <u>God-breathed</u> and is useful for teaching, rebuking, correcting and training in righteousness, so that the man of God may be thoroughly equipped for every good work.* (2 Timothy 3:16–17 NIV)

> *For no prophecy was ever produced by the will of man, but men <u>spoke from God</u> as they were carried along by the Holy Spirit.* (2 Peter 1:21 ESV)

> *And we also thank God constantly for this, that when you received the word of God, which you heard from us, you accepted it not as the word*

of men but as what it really is, the <u>word of God</u>, which is at work in you believers. (1 Thessalonians 2:13 ESV)

The Bible has two major divisions, the Old Testament (thirty-nine books) and the New Testament (twenty-seven books). The Old Testament contains history, law, poetry, wisdom literature, and prophecy. It was given to the Jewish people from the time of their exodus from slavery in Egypt, thought to have been around 1450 BC, until about 425 BC. The New Testament contains the story of the life, death, and resurrection of Jesus Christ; the early growth of the Christian Church; letters written by the apostles and other early church leaders to educate and encourage believers; and prophecies about the end times.

Because both Jews and Christians believed the Scriptures to be the actual words of God, they took great care to ensure accuracy as copies were made and disseminated. The copies were checked multiple times, and even the number of characters was counted! If any errors were found, the copy was destroyed and the process was begun again.

The Bible was originally written in Hebrew, Aramaic, and Greek. Archaeological discoveries in recent times have unearthed older manuscripts than those used by early translators. When these manuscripts have been compared, no significant differences have been found. We can be very confident that the original-language manuscripts used today contain essentially the same information as the originals. This is why seminary students study Hebrew and Greek as part of their training. Of course, most of us don't know those original languages, so what about the Bible translations we read today?

Even before the time of Christ, Hebrew was no longer routinely spoken by the Jewish people, especially those not living in Israel. Greek was and is a very rich and expressive language, and it was known across the civilized world of that time thanks to the conquests of Alexander the Great; hence, it was the ideal language for the spread of Scripture. Around 250 BC, an Egyptian king gathered seventy-two translators, six from each of the twelve tribes of Israel, to translate the Hebrew Bible into Greek. This version is called the Septuagint (from the Latin word for *seventy*). Most of the New Testament was originally written in Greek.

To produce our English translations of the Bible, translators have used several different methodologies. "Formal" or "word-for-word" translations strive to make the target language version match as closely as possible the exact words of the original source version. Examples are the King James Version (KJV) and the New American Standard Bible (NASB). "Dynamic," "thought-for-thought," or "paraphrase" translations try to convey the meaning of the source version to its original audience—not only in the new target language but also in the way that language is currently understood by a modern audience. This method tries to compensate for changes in customs and environment, as well as changes in the languages themselves over time. Examples are the New Living Translation (NLT) and The Message (MSG). Other translations fall somewhere between these two extremes. Examples are the Holman Christian Standard Bible (HCSB) and the New International Version (NIV). Although we can be very confident that the essential content of the originals has not been lost, it can be helpful to read multiple translations because some may convey nuances of meaning that others may not. I'll be quoting from several versions, choosing the one that I believe best expresses the message I'm trying to get across.

Another reason for confidence in the content of our Bibles is that God Himself actively protects His Word from error! If, as I have argued earlier, the Bible is His way of communicating His rules and principles to us, it makes sense that He would make sure it remains accurate! As Scripture says:

> *Heaven and earth shall pass away, but my words shall not pass away.* (Matthew 24:35 KJV)

> *The grass withers, the flower fades, but the word of our God stands forever.* (Isaiah 40:8 NASU)

One of the greatest reasons we have for confidence that the Bible is in fact God's Word is the evidence of fulfilled prophecy. Although some of the prophecies in the Bible, particularly those in the book of Revelation, describe events that are still future, there are many prophecies that have already been fulfilled, often many years after they were predicted. In Daniel, the succession of world empires was described, and those prophecies have mostly been fulfilled, except for a few that refer to the end times. The prophet Isaiah predicted the actual name of the Persian king, Cyrus, who would allow the Israelites to return and rebuild Jerusalem after the Babylonian captivity – even though that captivity hadn't happened yet!

> *"I am the Lord ... who says of Jerusalem, 'She shall be inhabited,' and of the cities of Judah, 'They shall be built, and I will raise up their ruins'; ... who says of <u>Cyrus</u>, 'He is my shepherd, and he shall fulfill all my purpose'; saying of Jerusalem, 'She shall be built,' and of the temple, 'Your foundation shall be laid.'"* (Isaiah 44:24–44 ESV)

Alexander the Great, who conquered most of the known world, spared Jerusalem when the Jewish High Priest met him and showed him the prophecies of his conquests from the book of Daniel. (Alexander had also had a dream about a man dressed like the High Priest, who encouraged him to proceed to conquer the Persians.)

All the prophecies concerning Jesus's birth, life, death, and resurrection—and there are many—were fulfilled to the letter when He actually came. I'll talk more about some of these and other prophecies in later chapters.

WHAT THE BIBLE SAYS
ABOUT GOD

The Bible is all about God and His dealings with mankind, and we'll learn much more about God as we go along, but I want to concentrate for now on just a few of the characteristics of God as described in the Bible.

God is omnipotent (all-powerful):

> *I am the Lord! There is nothing too difficult for me.* (Genesis 18:14 CEV)

> *"Ah, Sovereign Lord, you have made the heavens and the earth by your great power and outstretched arm. Nothing is too hard for you."* (Jeremiah 32:17 NIV)

> *"For nothing will be impossible with God."* (Luke 1:37 NASU)

God is omnipresent (everywhere at once):

I am everywhere—both near and far, in heaven and on earth. There are no secret places where you can hide from me. (Jeremiah 23:23–24 CEV)

Where could I go to escape from you? Where could I get away from your presence? If I went up to heaven, you would be there; if I lay down in the world of the dead, you would be there. If I flew away beyond the east or lived in the farthest place in the west, you would be there to lead me, you would be there to help me. (Psalms 139:7–10 GNT)

God is omniscient (all-knowing):

He counts the number of the stars; He gives names to all of them. Great is our Lord and abundant in strength; His understanding is infinite. (Psalms 147:4–5 NASU)

Are not five sparrows sold for two pennies? Yet not one of them is forgotten by God. Indeed, the very hairs of your head are all numbered. (Luke 12:6–7 NIV)

God is not constrained by time:

I am God, and there is no one like Me, declaring the end from the beginning, and from ancient times things which have not been done. (Isaiah 46:9–10 NASU)

But do not forget this one thing, dear friends: With the Lord a day is like a thousand years, and a thousand years are like a day. (2 Peter 3:8 NIV)

God is unchanging:

"I the Lord do not change." (Malachi 3:6 NIV)

God does not lie. God is faithful and always keeps His promises:

God is no mere human! He doesn't tell lies or change his mind. God always keeps his promises. (Numbers 23:19 CEV)

If we are faithless, He remains faithful, for He cannot deny Himself. (2 Timothy 2:13 NASU)

God is holy (pure, set apart):

"Holy, holy, holy is the Lord God Almighty, who was, and is, and is to come." (Revelation 4:8 NIV)

And the Lord said ... "you cannot see my face, for no one may see me and live." (Exodus 33:19–20 NIV)

God is perfect, just, and righteous in all He does:

"His work is perfect, for all His ways are just; a God of faithfulness and without injustice, righteous and upright is He." (Deuteronomy 32:4 NASU)

"Will not the Judge of all the earth do right?" (Genesis 18:25 NIV)

God is merciful, gracious, compassionate, patient, and good:

The Lord is merciful and compassionate, slow to get angry and filled with unfailing love. The Lord is good to everyone. He showers compassion on all his creation. (Psalms 145:8–9 NLT)

The Lord is gracious and righteous; our God is full of compassion. (Psalms 116:5 NIV)

Yet the Lord longs to be gracious to you; he rises to show you compassion. For the Lord is a God of justice. (Isaiah 30:18 NIV)

And perhaps most important, God is love:

Whoever does not love does not know God, because God is love. This is how God showed his love among us: He sent his one and only Son into the world that we might live through him. (1 John 4:8–9 NIV)

As we will see in later chapters, the characteristics of God sometimes seem to clash (e.g., justice and mercy), but He always has a resolution for the conflict. Still, we humans cannot expect to completely understand God. God frequently does not (and does not have to) explain Himself to us. He gives us the information we need to know, not necessarily all that we might want to know!

"For My thoughts are not your thoughts, nor are your ways My ways," declares the Lord. "For as the heavens are higher than the earth, so are My ways higher than your ways, and My thoughts than your thoughts." (Isaiah 55:8–9 NASU)

Who can measure the wealth and wisdom and knowledge of God? Who can understand his decisions or explain what he does? (Romans 11:33 CEV)

Now all we can see of God is like a cloudy picture in a mirror. Later we will see him face to face. We don't know everything, but then we will, just as God completely understands us. (1 Corinthians 13:12 CEV)

THE TRINITY

As one example of something hard to understand about God, the Bible refers to God as one God, yet it also describes God as active in three Persons—God the Father, Jesus the Son, and the Holy Spirit! In some passages, God clearly uses the plural *us* to describe Himself.

Hear, O Israel: The Lord our God, the Lord is <u>one</u>. (Deuteronomy 6:4 NIV)

Then God said, "Let <u>us</u> make human beings in <u>our</u> image, to be like ourselves." (Genesis 1:26 NLT)

Come, let <u>us</u> go down and confuse their language so they will not understand each other. (Genesis 11:7 NIV)

And I heard the voice of the Lord saying, "Whom shall I send, and who will go for <u>us</u>?" (Isaiah 6:8 ESV)

[Jesus speaking] *"I and the Father are <u>one</u>."* (John 10:30 NIV)

The Lord said to my Lord, "Sit in the place of honor at my right hand until I humble your enemies, making them a footstool under your feet." (Psalms 110:1 NLT)

The grace of the Lord Jesus Christ, and the love of God, and the fellowship of the Holy Spirit, be with you all. (2 Corinthians 13:14 NASU)

This concept of God as "Three in One" is called the Trinity, and it is admittedly not an easy thing to understand!

I heard an illustration many years ago that helped me with this. Visualize a three-tined fork sticking through a piece of paper. From one side of the paper, representing our limited world of four dimensions (three-dimensional space and time), we see only the three tines symbolizing the Father, Son, and Holy Spirit. Yet from the other side of the paper (representing the unlimited heavenly point of view), we see that there is only one whole fork (representing God).

I know this illustration probably doesn't bear any resemblance at all to what the Trinity *actually* means, but it satisfied me enough at the time that I could accept it and move on. Over the years, as I have grown to believe that the Bible is truly the Word of God, these hard sayings don't really bother me anymore!

WHAT THE BIBLE SAYS
ABOUT ANGELS, DEMONS, AND SATAN

As He did with man, God created angelic beings with free will—they could choose to serve Him or not. Angels are mentioned throughout the Bible, but surprisingly only a few are actually mentioned by name. Gabriel appears to be a special messenger of God to the Jewish people. We know that he appeared personally to Daniel in the Old Testament (more than once); to Zechariah, the father of John the Baptist; and to Mary, the mother of Jesus:

> *While I, Daniel, was trying to make sense of what I was seeing, suddenly there was a humanlike figure standing before me. Then I heard a man's voice from over by the Ulai Canal calling out, 'Gabriel, tell this man what is going on. Explain the vision to him.' (Daniel 8:15–16 MSG)*

> *I was still confessing my sins and those of all Israel to the Lord my God, and I was praying*

for the good of his holy mountain, when Gabriel suddenly came flying in at the time of the evening sacrifice. This was the same Gabriel I had seen in my vision, and he explained: Daniel, I am here to help you understand the vision. God thinks highly of you, and at the very moment you started praying, I was sent to give you the answer. (Daniel 9:20–23 CEV)

And the angel answered him [Zechariah], *"I am Gabriel. I stand in the presence of God, and I was sent to speak to you and to bring you this good news."* (Luke 1:19 ESV)

In the sixth month, God sent the angel Gabriel to Nazareth, a town in Galilee, to a virgin pledged to be married to a man named Joseph, a descendant of David. The virgin's name was Mary. The angel went to her and said, "Greetings, you who are highly favored! The Lord is with you." (Luke 1:26–28 NIV)

Michael is another named angel. He is described as the guardian angel of Israel:

"Now at that time Michael, the great prince who stands guard over the sons of your people, will arise." (Daniel 12:1 NASU)

We'll see more about Michael shortly.

A third named angel is Lucifer (which means "Light Bearer"). His story is not a good one. He became prideful and rebelled against God. We now know him as *Satan* or the Devil:

This is what the Sovereign Lord says: "You were the model of perfection, full of wisdom and perfect in beauty. You were in Eden, the garden of God; every precious stone adorned you: ruby, topaz and emerald, chrysolite, onyx and jasper, sapphire, turquoise and beryl. Your settings and mountings were made of gold; ... You were anointed as a guardian cherub, for so I ordained you. You were on the holy mount of God; you walked among the fiery stones. You were blameless in your ways from the day you were created till wickedness was found in you ... So I drove you in disgrace from the mount of God, and I expelled you, O guardian cherub, from among the fiery stones. Your heart became proud on account of your beauty, and you corrupted your wisdom because of your splendor. So I threw you to the earth." (Ezekiel 28:11–17 NIV)

Satan means "Accuser", and that is what he continues to do today:

One day the angels came to present themselves before the Lord, and Satan also came with them. The Lord said to Satan, "Where have you come from?" Satan answered the Lord, "From roaming through the earth and going back and forth in it." (Job 1:6–7 NIV)

I was given another vision. This time Joshua the high priest was standing in front of the Lord's angel. And there was Satan, standing at Joshua's right side, ready to accuse him. (Zechariah 3:1 CEV)

Jesus said, "Simon, listen to me! Satan has demanded the right to test each one of you, as a farmer does when he separates wheat from the husks. But Simon, I have prayed that your faith will be strong. And when you have come back to me, help the others." (Luke 22:31–32 CEV)

As soon as Judas took the bread, Satan entered into him. (John 13:27 NIV)

Be self-controlled and alert. Your enemy the devil prowls around like a roaring lion looking for someone to devour. (1 Peter 5:8 NIV)

Not only did Satan rebel, but many other angels joined with him. These we know today as demons or evil spirits. Some of them are bound until the end times, whereas others roam the earth, tormenting and even possessing humans:

And the angels who did not keep their positions of authority but abandoned their own home—these he has kept in darkness, bound with everlasting chains for judgment on the great Day. (Jude 1:6 NIV)

When he saw Jesus from a distance, he ran and fell on his knees in front of him. He shouted at the top of his voice, "What do you want with me, Jesus, Son of the Most High God? Swear to God that you won't torture me!" For Jesus had said to him, "Come out of this man, you evil spirit!" Then Jesus asked him, "What is your name?" "My name is Legion," he replied, "for we are many." (Mark 5:6–9 NIV)

And when he [Jesus] came to the other side, to the country of the Gadarenes, two demon-possessed men met him, coming out of the tombs, so fierce that no one could pass that way. And behold, they cried out, "What have you to do with us, O Son of God? Have you come here to torment us before the time?" Now a herd of many pigs was feeding at some distance from them. And the demons begged him, saying, "If you cast us out, send us away into the herd of pigs." And he said to them, "Go." So they came out and went into the pigs, and behold, the whole herd rushed down the steep bank into the sea and drowned in the waters. (Matthew 8:28–32 ESV)

The Bible tells us that Satan and his demons have a hierarchy, and that many of our troubles are due to their work behind the scenes, running the world we live in:

Put on the full armor of God so that you can take your stand against the devil's schemes. For our struggle is not against flesh and blood, but against the rulers, against the authorities, against the powers of this dark world and against the spiritual forces of evil in the heavenly realms. (Ephesians 6:11–12 NIV)

Satan and his demons are always trying to deceive us:

He [Satan] has always been a murderer and a liar. There is nothing truthful about him. He speaks on his own, and everything he says is a lie. Not only is he a liar himself, but he is also the father of all lies. (John 8:44 CEV)

No wonder, for even Satan disguises himself as an angel of light. Therefore it is not surprising if his servants also disguise themselves as servants of righteousness, whose end will be according to their deeds. (2 Corinthians 11:14–15 NASU)

The demons also do battle with God's angels. Here again, we see Michael and Gabriel at work:

[Gabriel speaking] *Daniel, don't be afraid! God has listened to your prayers since the first day you humbly asked for understanding, and he has sent me here. But the guardian angel* [demon] *of Persia opposed me for twenty-one days. Then Michael, who is one of the strongest guardian angels, came to rescue me from the kings* [chief demons] *of Persia.* (Daniel 10:12–13 CEV)

Then the angel said: Now do you understand why I have come? Soon I must leave to fight against the guardian angel [demon] *of Persia. Then after I have defeated him, the guardian angel* [demon] *of Greece will attack me. I will tell you what is written in The Book of Truth. But first, you must realize that no one except Michael, the guardian angel of Israel, is on my side. You also need to know that I protected and helped Darius the Mede in his first year as king.* (Daniel 10:20–11:1 CEV)

When Adam, the first man, chose to disobey God (as we shall see later), he effectively handed the "title deed" of the Earth to Satan:

Satan, who is <u>the god of this world</u>, *has blinded the minds of those who don't believe.* (2 Corinthians 4:4 NLT)

The time for judging this world has come, when Satan, <u>the ruler of this world</u>, will be cast out. (John 12:31 NLT)

We are certain that we come from God and that <u>the rest of the world is under the power of the devil</u>. (1 John 5:19 CEV)

When Satan tempted Jesus at the beginning of His earthly ministry, he offered Him the kingdoms of this world:

And the devil took him up and showed him all the kingdoms of the world in a moment of time, and said to him, "To you I will give all this authority and their glory, for <u>it has been delivered to me, and I give it to whom I will</u>. If you, then, will worship me, it will all be yours." (Luke 4:5–7 ESV)

Because Jesus did not dispute the validity of Satan's offer, we must conclude that Satan could in fact have given the kingdoms to Him! No wonder the world we live in is filled with pain, decay, heartache, and disaster! It fell under a curse when Adam sinned:

Against its will, all creation was subjected to God's curse. (Romans 8:20 NLT)

This does not mean that God is no longer in control of what happens on Earth, but it does seem to indicate that God allows Satan to operate somewhat freely here, within limits. We see in the book of Job that Satan could not torment Job without God's permission. First, he was allowed to strike Job's family and possessions:

"Does Job fear God for nothing?" Satan replied. "Have you not put a hedge around him and his

household and everything he has? You have blessed
the work of his hands, so that his flocks and herds
are spread throughout the land. But stretch out
your hand and strike everything he has, and he
will surely curse you to your face." The Lord said
to Satan, "Very well, then, everything he has is in
your hands, but on the man himself do not lay a
finger." (Job 1:9–12 NIV)

Later, when Job still remained faithful to God, Satan was allowed to attack Job's body, but not to kill him:

Then Satan answered the Lord and said, "Skin for
skin! All that a man has he will give for his life. But
stretch out your hand and touch his bone and his
flesh, and he will curse you to your face." And the
Lord said to Satan, "Behold, he is in your hand;
only spare his life." So Satan went out from the
presence of the Lord and struck Job with loathsome
sores from the sole of his foot to the crown of his
head. (Job 2:4–7 ESV)

Satan and the curse on creation, as well as the choices of fallen humans, result in terrible things happening on this earth—both to good people and to bad people. Still, we know that God is good! Exactly why God allows tragedies on earth is one of those mysteries that we aren't going to fully understand until we get to Heaven. Satan uses this mystery to poison our minds against God, saying, "If God is so good, why does He allow these horrible things to happen?" Fortunately, God has a promise for those who love Him:

And we know that God causes all things to work
together for good to those who love God, to those

who are called according to His purpose. (Romans
8:28 NASU)

We have seen in the stories of Satan's accusations of Job and of
Joshua, the High Priest, that he apparently still has access to God
in Heaven. But the Bible tells us of his sin, and of his eventual end:

> *How art thou fallen from heaven, O Lucifer, son of
> the morning! How art thou cut down to the ground,
> which didst weaken the nations! For thou hast said
> in thine heart, I will ascend into heaven, I will
> exalt my throne above the stars of God: I will sit
> also upon the mount of the congregation, in the
> sides of the north: I will ascend above the heights
> of the clouds; I will be like the most High. Yet thou
> shalt be brought down to hell, to the sides of the pit.*
> (Isaiah 14:12–15 KJV)

> *And he* [Jesus] *said to them, "I saw Satan fall like
> lightning from heaven."* (Luke 10:18 ESV)

> *And there was war in heaven. Michael and his angels
> fought against the dragon, and the dragon and his
> angels fought back. But he was not strong enough,
> and they lost their place in heaven. The great dragon
> was hurled down—that ancient serpent called the
> devil, or Satan, who leads the whole world astray.
> He was hurled to the earth, and his angels with him.
> Then I heard a loud voice in heaven say: "Now have
> come the salvation and the power and the kingdom
> of our God, and the authority of his Christ. For the
> accuser of our brothers, who accuses them before
> our God day and night, has been hurled down."*
> (Revelation 12:7–10 NIV)

GUARDIAN ANGELS?

One final thing about angels. A common theme in popular culture is that we all have guardian angels. We have seen that the Bible says that nations may indeed have guardian angels (and demons!). The Bible sometimes depicts angels at work in the lives of people, but there is nothing in the Bible that says we each have one of our own or that they stand guard over us as individuals.

However, Jesus himself said that little children do indeed have guardian angels!

> Beware that you don't look down on any of these little ones. For I tell you that in heaven their angels are always in the presence of my heavenly Father. (Matthew 18:10 NLT)

WHAT THE BIBLE SAYS
ABOUT MAN, AND
THE PROBLEM OF SIN

God formed Adam, the first man, from the dust of the earth and breathed into him the breath of life. He later took a rib from Adam and formed the first woman, Eve, as his helpmate. These first humans lived in the garden of Eden, a perfect environment, and had close fellowship with God. They were created with free will—they could choose to obey God, or not. Adam and Eve were given only one rule to follow:

> *The Lord God commanded the man, saying, "From any tree of the garden you may eat freely; but from the tree of the knowledge of good and evil you shall not eat, for in the day that you eat from it you will surely die." (Genesis 2:16–17 NASU)*

Sure enough, under the temptation of Satan, they managed to break that one rule. Although they could have lived forever under God's blessing, their sin brought death into the world. It was not only spiritual death, which happened immediately, but physical death, which happened later. Even the creation itself suffered a curse. Unfortunately, all of us have inherited their sin, and the sentence of death:

> *Adam sinned, and that sin brought death into the world. Now everyone has sinned, and so everyone must die ... This happened, though not everyone disobeyed a direct command from God, as Adam did.* (Romans 5:12–14 CEV)

> *The creation looks forward to the day when it will join God's children in glorious freedom from death and decay. For we know that all creation has been groaning as in the pains of childbirth right up to the present time.* (Romans 8:21–22 NLT)

We may think "Well, if it had been me instead of Adam, I would not have sinned!" But the Bible says otherwise. Because of Adam's sin, we are all born with a sin nature:

> *For all have sinned and fall short of the glory of God.* (Romans 3:23 HCSB)

> *We are all infected and impure with sin.* (Isaiah 64:6 NLT)

> *If we say that we have no sin, we are deceiving ourselves and the truth is not in us.* (1 John 1:8 NASU)

> *As it is written, There is none righteous, no, not one ...* (Romans 3:10 KJV)

> *No one is good except God alone.* (Luke 18:19 NASU)

Adam's sin created a dilemma. He was now separated from God and could not have the kind of fellowship with Him that he had before. Plus, he was going to die! How could his relationship with God be repaired? Was there no hope?

Of course, this was not a dilemma for God. Being omniscient, He already knew it would happen, and already had a solution planned! This solution was revealed over a period of many centuries, but the essence of it was immediately obvious. The first death occurred at the hand of God, and the first blood was shed:

> *And the Lord God made clothing from animal skins for Adam and his wife.* (Genesis 3:21 NLT)

As later Bible writers would put it:

> *Without the shedding of blood there is no forgiveness of sins.* (Hebrews 9:22 ESV)

Thus began the sordid history of man and sin. I'll briefly overview what followed.

Men quickly became so evil that God destroyed almost all of them with a global flood; only Noah and his family were saved in the Ark. After this, man spread across the earth again, once again doing evil. God chose a man named Abram (whom He renamed Abraham), to be the one through whose descendants He would eventually redeem us. God made three key promises to Abraham: many descendants, a homeland, and one that is still very relevant to us today:

> *"All the families on earth will be blessed through you."* (Genesis 12:3 NLT)

As Abraham continued his sojourn with God, he often sinned, like everyone else. Still, he learned to believe God, which was all-important to Him:

> Consider Abraham: "He believed God, and it was credited to him as righteousness." (Galatians 3:6 NIV)

As we see, it was Abraham's *belief* in God, not his works or his sacrifices, which God rewarded!

It was not through all of Abraham's descendants, but through those of his son Isaac and grandson Jacob, that God's promises to Abraham would be fulfilled. Jacob, whose name God changed to Israel, had twelve sons, one of whom was Joseph. Jacob sinned by loving Joseph more than his brothers, and they responded by selling Joseph into slavery in Egypt. They lied to their father, letting him believe that Joseph had died.

Joseph spent years in servitude in Egypt, then more years in prison. Yet after God gave him the interpretation of Pharaoh's dream, he rose to a position of high prominence in Egypt, second only to Pharaoh himself. Through his God-given wisdom, he saved the Egyptians and other surrounding peoples from death by famine, including his father Jacob, his brothers, and his entire family—some seventy people in all. At the time, they were called Hebrews.

Later Pharaohs turned against the Hebrews and enslaved them for hundreds of years. During their time in slavery, they grew to become a nation of about six hundred thousand men, plus women and children. In God's time, He raised up Moses (a Hebrew raised as a prince of Egypt) to deliver them from slavery with signs and wonders. God gave them the Ten Commandments and a complete set of laws, instructions, and regulations. But by the time Moses came down from the mountain with the stone tablets of the law, written by the very finger of God, the Israelites had already made a golden calf and were worshipping it!

The Israelites' journey was a continual cycle of rebellion, disobedience, chastisement, and rescue. During one of these cycles, the following events happened:

> *Then the Lord sent fiery serpents among the people, and they bit the people, so that many people of Israel died. And the people came to Moses and said, "We have sinned, for we have spoken against the Lord and against you. Pray to the Lord, that he take away the serpents from us." So Moses prayed for the people. And the Lord said to Moses, "Make a fiery serpent and set it on a pole, and everyone who is bitten, when he sees it, shall live." So Moses made a bronze serpent and set it on a pole. And if a serpent bit anyone, he would look at the bronze serpent and live.* (Numbers 21:6–9 ESV)

We see in this example that all the people had to do was believe in what the Lord said, and He delivered them from death! This story will come up again in a later chapter.

Remember that as far back as Adam, the shedding of blood was necessary payment for the people's sins. God's instructions to the Israelites called for a system of daily animal sacrifices, as well as other offerings. These had to be performed according to very detailed and strict requirements.

> *Life is in the blood, and I have given you the blood of animals to sacrifice in place of your own.* (Leviticus 17:11 CEV)

Despite being singled out by God to become His covenant people and receive His favor, the children of Israel continued to rebel, and God continued to chastise them. When the people refused to enter the Promised Land because of their unbelief, the Lord forced them to wander in the wilderness for forty more years, until that unbelieving generation died. It was the following generation, under the leadership of Joshua, that conquered the existing inhabitants and took over the Promised Land (though never completely). Still, the cycle of rebellion, disobedience, chastisement, and rescue continued—first through the period of the Judges and then the period of the Kings. Israel flourished for a while under King David and his son Solomon, yet both of them sinned and were chastised.

Under subsequent kings, Israel broke apart into the two divided kingdoms, Judah (along with Benjamin) in the south and Israel (the rest of the tribes) in the north. At times, it appeared that the entire nation would be lost to God. Even the great prophet Elijah, in the northern kingdom, fell into a deep depression, thinking he was all alone in his faith in God:

> *He* [Elijah] *said, "I have been very jealous for the Lord, the God of hosts. For the people of Israel have forsaken your covenant, thrown down your altars, and killed your prophets with the sword, and I, even I only, am left, and they seek my life, to take it away."* (1 Kings 19:10 ESV)

But God informed Elijah otherwise!

> *"Yet I reserve seven thousand in Israel—all whose knees have not bowed down to Baal and all whose mouths have not kissed him."* (1 Kings 19:18 NIV)

Noah and his family were a very small remnant out of all those living at the time of the flood. Seven thousand in Israel in Elijah's time, out of probably millions, was a very small remnant as well. But no matter how bleak things may appear, God always maintains a remnant!

Following this, both Israel and later Judah were taken into exile, as they were promised would happen if they refused to keep the covenant they had made with God. Judah was taken captive to Babylon, and Jerusalem was destroyed. (The Israelites were by that time called the Jews, after the kingdom and tribe of Judah.) Still, even in exile, God protected His remnant. Although the temple sacrifices ceased, God let His people know through His prophets that by faith, He could still save them.

> *I'd rather for you to be faithful and to know me than to offer sacrifices.* (Hosea 6:6 CEV)

> *O Lord, open my lips, and my mouth will declare your praise. You do not delight in sacrifice, or I would bring it; you do not take pleasure in burnt offerings. The sacrifices of God are a broken spirit; a broken and contrite heart, O God, you will not despise.* (Psalms 51:15–17 NIV)

> *I will praise the name of God with a song; I will magnify him with thanksgiving. This will please the Lord more than an ox or a bull with horns and hoofs.* (Psalms 69:30–31 ESV)

Seventy years after Judah's exile to Babylon, Cyrus gave his prophesied proclamation allowing the Jews to return to Jerusalem, rebuild the Temple, and resume sacrifices.

God taught the Israelites many things through Moses and the prophets. Among the things they learned was that God's law, though good, was impossible for man to keep!

> *For no one can ever be made right with God by doing what the law commands. The law simply shows us how sinful we are.* (Romans 3:20 NLT)

> *Because by the works of the law no human being will be justified.* (Galatians 2:16 HCSB)

Also, although blood sacrifices could temporarily cover their sins, such sacrifices could not entirely take away their sins:

> *But those sacrifices are an annual reminder of sins, because it is impossible for the blood of bulls and goats to take away sins.* (Hebrews 10:3–4 NIV)

Still, God had His plan in place, and it was about to come to fruition. The prophets foretold of the One to come Who would solve the problem of sin once and for all, lead Israel to prominence in the world, and completely fulfill all the promises God gave to Abraham, Isaac, and Jacob, including ultimately

> *"All the families on earth will be blessed through you."* (Genesis 12:3 NLT)

Less than a hundred years after the remnant of Jewish exiles returned to Jerusalem, the prophets went silent. After the prophecies of Malachi, around 425 BC, the Old Testament writings were closed, and the people of God eagerly waited to see what He would do next!

IS THERE ANYTHING GOD CAN'T DO?

We know that God is omnipotent (all-powerful), so there is nothing He can't do, from the standpoint of His ability and power. But there are things that He can't (or won't) do, because doing them would be inconsistent with His nature. For example, the Bible emphatically says:

It is impossible for God to lie. (Hebrews 6:18 NASU)

God also cannot interfere with the free will of His created beings. God cannot make a wayward spouse or child return, although He can trouble their conscience. God cannot force our loved ones to believe in Him, although He can create opportunities for them to be presented with the gospel.

Most important, even though He loves us dearly, God cannot allow us sinners into Heaven by any "back door" method. That would be unjust, and God cannot be unjust. The death penalty for sin must be paid! Thankfully, Christ has already paid that penalty for us, and we only have to believe that and accept what He did by faith.

We may enter Heaven *only* by the path He has provided—by trusting in His Son, the Lord Jesus Christ!

6

WHAT THE BIBLE SAYS
ABOUT JESUS, THE
SOLUTION FOR SIN

Writing a brief chapter or two about Jesus is a daunting task. One of His closest disciples on earth, the apostle John, said:

> *Jesus did many other things as well. If every one of them were written down, I suppose that even the whole world would not have room for the books that would be written.* (John 21:25 NIV)

Obviously, I can't begin to relate everything Jesus did in a few pages! Again, I hope to encourage you to read what the Bible says about Him for yourself!

The Old Testament contains many prophecies about the coming Messiah. Some describe his lowly birth to a virgin in Bethlehem:

> *"Therefore the Lord Himself will give you a sign: Behold, a virgin will be with child and bear a*

son, and she will call His name Immanuel [which means, 'God with us']." (Isaiah 7:14 NASU)

"But as for you, Bethlehem Ephrathah, too little to be among the clans of Judah, from you One will go forth for Me to be ruler in Israel. His goings forth are from long ago, from the days of eternity." (Micah 5:2 NASU)

Others gave hints as to how His life on earth would unfold:

Out of Egypt I called my son. [Joseph, Mary, and Jesus fled to Egypt for a time to escape Herod.] (Hosea 11:1 NIV)

In earlier times He treated the land of Zebulun and the land of Naphtali with contempt, but later on He shall make it glorious, by the way of the sea, on the other side of Jordan, Galilee of the Gentiles. The people who walk in darkness will see a great light; those who live in a dark land, the light will shine on them. [Jesus grew up in Nazareth, and He lived and taught in Galilee.] (Isaiah 9:1–2 NASU)

Even my close friend in whom I trusted, who ate my bread, has lifted his heel against me. [Judas, one of His twelve disciples, betrayed Him.] (Psalms 41:9 ESV)

Many of the Old Testament prophecies depict His coming in glory and power as the "Conquering Messiah":

For to us a child is born, to us a son is given, and the government will be on his shoulders. And he will be called Wonderful Counselor, Mighty God, Everlasting Father, Prince of Peace. Of the increase of his government and peace there will be no end. He will reign on David's throne and over his kingdom, establishing and upholding it with justice and righteousness from that time on and forever. (Isaiah 9:6–7 NIV)

But other prophecies describe a meek and humble Messiah who would endure torture, suffering, and death—not for His own sins, but for ours! The following excerpt from Isaiah 53 is an amazingly rich and accurate description of the "Suffering Servant":

The servant grew up obeying the Lord. He wasn't some handsome king. Nothing about the way he looked made him attractive to us. He was hated and rejected; his life was filled with sorrow and terrible suffering. No one wanted to look at him. We despised him and said, "He is a nobody!" He suffered and endured great pain for us, but we thought his suffering was punishment from God. He was wounded and crushed because of our sins; by taking our punishment, he made us completely well. All of us were like sheep that had wandered off. We had each gone our own way, but the Lord gave him the punishment we deserved. He was painfully abused, but he did not complain. He was silent like a lamb being led to the butcher, as quiet as a sheep having its wool cut off. He was condemned to death without a fair trial. Who could have imagined what would happen to him? His life was taken away because of the sinful things my people had done. He wasn't dishonest or violent, but he was buried in a tomb of cruel and rich people. The

Lord decided his servant would suffer as a sacrifice to take away the sin and guilt of others. Now the servant will live to see his own descendants. He did everything the Lord had planned. By suffering, the servant will learn the true meaning of obeying the Lord. Although he is innocent, he will take the punishment for the sins of others, so that many of them will no longer be guilty. The Lord will reward him with honor and power for sacrificing his life. Others thought he was a sinner, but he suffered for our sins and asked God to forgive us. (Isaiah 53: 2–12 CEV)

Religious scholars struggled with how all these prophecies could be true about a single person. Most failed to see that Messiah would come twice, first to suffer and die in payment for our sins, but also to rise again bodily, ascend to Heaven, and later return a second time as conqueror and judge!

Israel in New Testament times was oppressed by the Romans, who ruled them with an iron fist. The Jews desperately wanted the "Conquering Messiah" to come, overthrow the Romans, and establish Israel in their rightful place as head of the nations, as God had promised. But around 6 BC by today's calendar, God had something altogether different in mind! He sent his one and only Son to earth as a baby!

Let's first look at what the Bible says about who Jesus is. First, He is God, the Son of God. He is the Creator! He did not begin His life in a stable in Bethlehem but has always existed. He took on human form and was born of a virgin—He had no human father. He is both fully God and fully man. He is the Messiah, the Christ, the Lamb of God, and our High Priest:

The angel replied, "The Holy Spirit will come upon you, and the power of the Most High will overshadow you. So the baby to be born will be holy, and he will be called <u>the Son of God</u>." (Luke 1:35–36 NLT)

After being baptized, Jesus came up immediately from the water; and behold, the heavens were opened, and he saw the Spirit of God descending as a dove and lighting on Him, and behold, a voice out of the heavens said, "<u>This is My beloved Son</u>, in whom I am well-pleased." (Matthew 3:16–17 NASU)

Everything was created by him, everything in heaven and on earth, everything seen and unseen, including all forces and powers, and all rulers and authorities. <u>All things were created by God's Son</u>, and everything was made for him. (Colossians 1:16 CEV)

For in Christ lives <u>all the fullness of God in a human body</u>. (Colossians 2:9 NLT)

The next day John saw Jesus coming toward him and said, "Look! The <u>Lamb of God</u> who takes away the sin of the world!" (John 1:29 NLT)

The woman said, "I know that Messiah" (called Christ) "is coming. When he comes, he will explain everything to us." Then Jesus declared, "<u>I who speak to you am he</u>." (John 4:25–26 NIV)

Because God's children are human beings—made of flesh and blood—<u>the Son also became flesh and</u>

blood. *For only as a human being could he die, and only by dying could he break the power of the devil, who had the power of death. Only in this way could he set free all who have lived their lives as slaves to the fear of dying.* (Hebrews 2:14–15 NLT)

Therefore, it was necessary for him to be made in every respect like us, his brothers and sisters, so that he could be our merciful and faithful <u>High Priest</u> before God. Then he could offer a sacrifice that would take away the sins of the people. (Hebrews 2:17 NLT)

Though he was God, he did not think of equality with God as something to cling to. Instead, he gave up his divine privileges; he took the humble position of a slave and was born as a human being. When he appeared in human form, he humbled himself in obedience to God and died a criminal's death on a cross. (Philippians 2:6–8 NLT)

Next, we'll look at what the Bible says about why Jesus came. He came to fulfill the Law; He came to show us what God is really like; He came to teach us that we need a Savior; and most important, he came to become that Savior by dying on a Roman cross to pay the penalty for your sins and mine!

"Do not think that I have come to abolish the Law or the Prophets; I have not come to abolish them but to fulfill them." (Matthew 5:17 ESV)

For Christ has already accomplished the purpose for which the law was given. As a result, all who believe in him are made right with God. (Romans 10:4 NLT)

In the past God spoke to our forefathers through the prophets at many times and in various ways, but in these last days he has spoken to us by his Son, whom he appointed heir of all things, and through whom he made the universe. (Hebrews 1:1–2 NIV)

For God so loved the world that he gave his one and only Son, that whoever believes in him shall not perish but have eternal life. For God did not send his Son into the world to condemn the world, but to save the world through him. (John 3:16–17 NIV)

He who has seen Me has seen the Father; … Do you not believe that I am in the Father, and the Father is in Me? The words that I say to you I do not speak on My own initiative, but the Father abiding in Me does His works. Believe Me that I am in the Father and the Father is in Me. (John 14:9–11 NASU)

No one has ever seen God. But the one and only Son is himself God and is near to the Father's heart. He has revealed God to us. (John 1:18 NLT)

"I and the Father are one." (John 10:30 NIV)

"For even the Son of Man did not come to be served, but to serve, and to give his life as a ransom for many." (Mark 10:45 NIV)

"For the Son of Man came to seek and to save the lost." (Luke 19:10 ESV)

*The saying is trustworthy and deserving of full
acceptance, that Christ Jesus came into the world
to save sinners.* (1 Timothy 1:15 ESV)

So what does the Bible say about what Jesus did? Let's look at just
a few things!

During His three-year ministry, he performed *many* miracles!
The Bible describes only a few of His healings of the blind, the
lame, and the sick, as well as His casting out demons from some
who were possessed. It also tells of a few material or physical
miracles, such as changing water into wine, calming stormy
seas, and feeding thousands with handfuls of bread and fish.
The Bible also mentions three occasions where He raised dead
people back to life! I want to emphasize, though, that it wasn't
just these few recorded miracles that Jesus performed. He healed
multitudes!

> *A great multitude of people from all Judea and
> Jerusalem ... came to hear him and to be healed
> of their diseases. And those who were troubled
> with unclean spirits were cured. And all the crowd
> sought to touch him, for power came out from him
> and healed them all.* (Luke 6:17–19 ESV)

In fact, Jesus's miracles were the primary way that He demonstrated
who He was:

> *The Jews gathered around him, saying, "How long
> will you keep us in suspense? If you are the Christ,
> tell us plainly." Jesus answered, "I did tell you, but
> you do not believe. The miracles I do in my Father's
> name speak for me, but you do not believe ... I and
> the Father are one."* (John 10:24–30 NIV)

42

I want to focus now on His teaching us of our need for a Savior, and how He fulfilled that very need.

We have already seen that the laws given to the Israelites through Moses were impossible for man to keep. But Jesus made this problem even worse! He taught that it wasn't just the things we do that are sinful, but also the impure thoughts we have, even if we don't act on them!

> *"You have heard that it was said to the people long ago, 'Do not murder, and anyone who murders will be subject to judgment.' But I tell you that anyone who is angry with his brother will be subject to judgment."* (Matthew 5:21–22 NIV)

> *"You have heard that it was said, 'Do not commit adultery.' But I tell you that anyone who looks at a woman lustfully has already committed adultery with her in his heart."* (Matthew 5:27–28 NIV)

Also, we sin when we don't do something that we know we should; these are called sins of omission:

> *Remember, it is sin to know what you ought to do and then not do it.* (James 4:17, NLT)

Now we are really in big trouble! Even if we think we are living pretty good lives, and that doing so will get us into Heaven, Jesus told us that we are very wrong!

> *For no one can ever be made right with God by doing what the law commands. The law simply shows us how sinful we are.* (Romans 3:20 NLT)

Not a single person on earth is always good and never sins. (Ecclesiastes 7:20 NLT)

Nothing impure will ever enter it [Heaven], nor will anyone who does what is shameful or deceitful, but only those whose names are written in the Lamb's book of life. (Revelation 21:27 NIV)

For I tell you that unless your righteousness surpasses that of the Pharisees and the teachers of the law, you will certainly not enter the kingdom of heaven. (Matthew 5:20 NIV)

Jesus answered and said to him, "Truly, truly, I say to you, unless one is born again he cannot see the kingdom of God." (John 3:3 NASU)

So how can we possibly measure up to God's standards? We'll get much deeper into this in a later chapter, but for now, let's look at just a few passages, including probably the most famous verse in the entire Bible:

For God so loved the world that he gave his one and only Son, that whoever <u>believes</u> in him shall not perish but have eternal life. For God did not send his Son into the world to condemn the world, but to save the world through him. Whoever <u>believes</u> in him is not condemned, but whoever does not believe stands condemned already because he has not believed in the name of God's one and only Son. (John 3:16–18 NIV)

"I tell you the truth, whoever hears my word and <u>believes</u> him who sent me has eternal life and will

not be condemned; he has crossed over from death to life." (John 5:24 NIV)

Then they asked him, "What must we do to do the works God requires?" Jesus answered, "The work of God is this: to <u>believe</u> in the one he has sent." (John 6:28–29 NIV)

I tell you for certain that everyone who <u>has faith</u> in me has eternal life. (John 6:47 CEV)

Can it really be that simple? Yes! Remember the story of the bronze serpent on a pole? The Israelites simply had to *believe* and look upon that bronze snake, and they would be saved from the actual snakes' venom. Jesus Himself said that this story was an illustration of what He was going to do when He was crucified:

Just as Moses lifted up the snake in the wilderness, so the Son of Man must be lifted up, so that everyone who believes in Him will have eternal life. (John 3:14–15 HCSB)

"When I am lifted up from the earth, I will draw everyone to me." (In saying this he indicated the kind of death he was going to suffer.) (John 12:32–33 GNT)

Really? That's all? What about baptism? What about sacrifice? What about prayer, Bible study, and service? What about tithes and giving? All those things are good, but they do not get us into Heaven. The best proof of this is the story of the thief on the cross next to Jesus. He at first cursed and taunted Jesus. But later, he admitted that he deserved the punishment he was suffering. He believed that Jesus was innocent, that He would not stay dead, and that He was Who He said He was. They had a very brief conversation, in which Jesus made an amazing statement:

> *Then he [the thief] said, "Jesus, remember me when you come into your kingdom." Jesus answered him, "I tell you the truth, today you will be with me in paradise." (Luke 23:42–43 NIV)*

Jesus said, "*Today* you will be with me in Paradise"! The thief had no opportunity to do anything after he believed! All he did, and all he could do, was *believe*!

Of course, Jesus's death on the cross was by no means the end of His story. On the third day after He was buried, He arose from the dead in a new yet physical, recognizable body that could eat, drink, walk, and talk (as well as go through walls and travel from one place to another instantly)! The resurrection was the final proof that God the Father had accepted the sacrifice that Jesus had made!

> *But the angel said to the women, "Do not be afraid, for I know that you seek Jesus who was crucified. He is not here, for he has risen, as he said. Come, see the place where he lay. Then go quickly and tell his disciples that he has risen from the dead, and behold, he is going before you to Galilee; there you will see him. See, I have told you." (Matthew 28:5–7 ESV)*

The apostle Paul wrote:

> *For what I received I passed on to you as of first importance: that Christ died for our sins according to the Scriptures, that he was buried, that he was*

raised on the third day according to the Scriptures, and that he appeared to Peter, and then to the Twelve. After that, he appeared to more than five hundred of the brothers at the same time, most of whom are still living, though some have fallen asleep. Then he appeared to James, then to all the apostles, and last of all he appeared to me also. (1 Corinthians 15:3–8 NIV)

Forty days after His resurrection, He ascended into Heaven, sat down at the right hand of the Father, and began serving as our High Priest, which He continues to do to this day:

Jesus said to them, " ... the Holy Spirit will come upon you and give you power. Then you will tell everyone about me in Jerusalem, in all Judea, in Samaria, and everywhere in the world." After Jesus had said this and while they were watching, he was taken up into a cloud. They could not see him, but as he went up, they kept looking up into the sky. Suddenly two men dressed in white clothes were standing there beside them. They said, "Why are you men from Galilee standing here and looking up into the sky? Jesus has been taken to heaven. But he will come back in the same way that you have seen him go." (Acts 1:7–11 CEV)

Christ Jesus is the one who died—more than that, who was raised—who is at the right hand of God, who indeed is interceding for us. (Romans 8:34 ESV)

So then, since we have a great High Priest who has entered heaven, Jesus the Son of God, let us hold firmly to what we believe. This High Priest of ours understands our weaknesses, for he faced all of the same testings we do, yet he did not sin. (Hebrews 4:14–15 NLT)

Before He left, He gave His disciples (including us) His marching orders:

Therefore go and make disciples of all nations, baptizing them in the name of the Father and of the Son and of the Holy Spirit, and teaching them to obey everything I have commanded you. (Matthew 28:19–20 NIV)

After His ascension, He sent the Holy Spirit, as He had promised. We'll learn more about the Holy Spirit in a later chapter.

THE FOUR GOSPELS

Because the good news (or the gospel) of Jesus Christ is so important, the New Testament actually contains four versions of it! The three so-called synoptic gospels were focused on communicating the gospel of Jesus to three different audiences of the day. Matthew was written for the Jews, the religious people already familiar with the Hebrew Scriptures (our Old Testament), and describes how Jesus fulfilled all the Old Testament prophecies about the coming Messiah (*Christ* is the Greek word for the Hebrew term *Messiah*). Mark was written for the Romans, strong men who respected strength, and emphasizes Jesus's power and ability. The gospel of Luke (who was a doctor) was written for the Greeks, the learned, intellectual, and scientific minds of the day, and is the most complete, analytic, and detailed depiction of Jesus as both God and perfect man. The fourth gospel, John, while written in extremely simple language, reaches to the heights and depths of spiritual truths, from eternity past to eternity future. It is intended primarily for people who already believe in Jesus, to help us grow. Of course, all four gospels are valuable for us today.

Of the eighty-nine chapters in the four gospels, eighty-five of them describe the last three years of His earthly journey. Of those eighty-five chapters, twenty-seven cover the last eight days! Considering this, it's obvious that the primary emphasis of the gospels is on Jesus's ministry, and especially on His death, burial, and resurrection!

WHAT ELSE DOES THE BIBLE SAY
ABOUT SALVATION?

Why do we need salvation?

The Bible teaches that we are eternal beings. Our lives do not end when our earthly bodies die:

> *We die only once, and then we are judged.* (Hebrews 9:27–28 CEV)

> *These will go away into eternal punishment, but the righteous into eternal life.* (Matthew 25:46 NASU)

These verses refute both the popular theories of death as "the end" (i.e., we just go nowhere, into nothingness) and of reincarnation.

We will spend eternity either in Heaven (eternal life with God) or in Hell (eternal torment, in separation from God). Don't be confused that when the Bible uses the term *eternal life* to refer to life with God in Heaven, that the alternative is just death—it's still an eternal existence, just not one that you would probably want for yourself or your loved ones. (I would personally be very happy if those who didn't go to Heaven just ceased to exist, but that is not what the Bible teaches.)

> *He will punish those who do not know God and do not obey the gospel of our Lord Jesus. They will be punished with everlasting destruction and shut out from the presence of the Lord and from the majesty of his power.* (2 Thessalonians 1:8–9 NIV)

> *But for the ... unbelieving ... and immoral ... and all liars, their part will be in the lake that burns with fire and brimstone, which is the second death.* (Revelation 21:8 NASU)

God loves you and wants you to spend eternity in Heaven with Him:

> *He is patient with you, not wanting anyone to perish, but everyone to come to repentance.* (2 Peter 3:9 NIV)

God Himself has provided the way to make that happen, and He has shown it to us in His word:

> *Jesus answered, "I am the way and the truth and the life. No one comes to the Father except through me."* (John 14:6 NIV)

What we do on earth determines where we will spend eternity. Actually, it's not what we do, but Whom we decide to believe in. Making the decision whether or not to believe in Jesus Christ is the most important thing you will do on this earth! Don't ignore that decision, and make it today! The Bible says that not deciding is the same as not believing—and you have no assurance that you will have another opportunity!

> *Whoever believes in him is not condemned, but whoever does not believe stands condemned already because he has not believed in the name of God's one and only Son.* (John 3:18 NIV)

> *"Today when you hear his voice, don't harden your hearts as Israel did when they rebelled."* (Hebrews 3:15 NLT)

> *You should know better than to say, "Today or tomorrow we will go to the city. We will do business there for a year and make a lot of money!" What do you know about tomorrow? How can you be so sure about your life? It is nothing more than mist that appears for only a little while before it disappears.* (James 4:13–14 CEV)

I hope that you will learn from the Bible what God wants you to do, but He will not force you. You must make that choice for yourself. It doesn't matter what your parents did or what your spouse does. It doesn't matter how much money or time you give to help the poor, serve others, or save the environment. It doesn't matter what church you may have joined or grew up in. It doesn't even really matter if you walked down the church aisle or raised your hand in a service. It matters Whom you believe in, Whom you are trusting in to save you. That is what salvation is all about!

When you trust in Jesus Christ, you are saved!

Before we look in more detail at how we are saved, let's look a bit more at how we are not saved. Religions around the world all tell us what we must do to be saved. Christianity, on the other hand, tells us about what God did to save us! The popular concept that if the sum of our good deeds outweighs the sum of our bad deeds we will go to Heaven is totally unbiblical! Salvation is the free gift of God!

> *God saved you by his grace when you believed. And you can't take credit for this; it is a gift from God. Salvation is not a reward for the good things we have done, so none of us can boast about it.* (Ephesians 2:8–9 NLT)

> *Money paid to workers isn't a gift. It is something they earn by working. But you cannot make God accept you because of something you do. God accepts sinners only because they have faith in him.* (Romans 4:4–5 CEV)

> *For they don't understand God's way of making people right with himself. Refusing to accept God's way, they cling to their own way of getting right with God by trying to keep the law. For Christ has already accomplished the purpose for which the law was given. As a result, all who believe in him are made right with God.* (Romans 10:3–4 NLT)

> *We are all infected and impure with sin. When we display our righteous deeds, they are nothing but filthy rags.* (Isaiah 64:6 NLT)

So then how are we to be saved? Some of the verses most often used to answer this question are as follows:

If you confess with your mouth, "Jesus is Lord," and believe in your heart that God raised him from the dead, you will be saved. (Romans 10:9 NIV)

I have had one message for Jews and Greeks alike— the necessity of repenting from sin and turning to God, and of having faith in our Lord Jesus. (Acts 20:21 NLT)

Repent therefore, and turn back, that your sins may be blotted out … (Acts 3:19 ESV)

Jesus answered and said to him, "Truly, truly, I say to you, unless one is born again he cannot see the kingdom of God." (John 3:3 NASU)

The jailer … asked, "Sirs, what must I do to be saved?" They replied, "Believe in the Lord Jesus, and you will be saved." (Acts 16:29–31 NIV)

We see words like *faith, belief, born again,* and *repent.* How do we make sense of all this? In some ways, they are different aspects of the same thing. Salvation must be simple enough for everyone to understand, but people have a natural tendency to try to make it more complicated than it really is.

Much wiser people than I have distilled it down to something like this:

1. Agree with God that you are a sinner, and that you can do nothing to save yourself.
2. Repent of (or turn from) your sins, and turn to God.
3. Believe that Jesus is the eternal Son of God; that He came to earth as a baby, born of a virgin; that He lived a sinless

life; that He died to pay the penalty for your sins; and that God raised Him from the dead as proof that His sacrifice was accepted.

4. Invite Him to be your Savior. Surrender your life to Him, and ask Him to be your Lord.
5. Trust your life to Jesus. Believe that He will save you, as He has promised. (This is having faith in Him.)

Then, after you have been saved:

6. Thank Him for dying for you, and for the free gift of salvation!
7. Tell someone! Confess to others that you have accepted Christ.[2]
8. Begin a lifestyle of following Christ. Read your Bible, pray, worship, and find a local church home where you can share your journey, helping and being helped by other believers.[3]

---

[2] Being baptized in water is the traditionally accepted method for making a public confession of faith, and we are in fact commanded in Scripture to be baptized after salvation. But as we saw in the story of the thief on the cross, the inability of a person to be baptized does not mean he is not saved.

[3] I really wish this warning was not necessary, but you must exercise a degree of caution when looking for a church home. There are many so-called churches out there that have some very unbiblical beliefs and teachings. If they don't have such basic beliefs as that the Bible is the Word of God; that Jesus is the Son of God; and that He lived a sinless life, died to pay the penalty for your sins, and was bodily resurrected, or if they teach that you have to do certain things other than believe in order to be saved, or if they teach that God will make you rich or heal your body if you just "believe enough" or give them money—run away! There are plenty of sound, biblically based churches out there, and they will be happy to give you a statement of their beliefs. Hopefully you have some Christian friends who can help you with your search. Ask God to help you, to let your spirit know whether you're in a good place or a bad place. Don't hesitate to make a change if you discover you made a mistake!

Trust (or faith or belief) is not just intellectual acceptance, but is firm reliance. An illustration often used is that of a chair. You may think it will hold your weight, but you don't really trust it until you sit down! Also, like the chair, faith always has an object. You must have faith in something or someone—in the case of salvation, that object is Jesus Christ. It is in Christ that you put your faith, and that is a solid foundation!

If you want to believe but are struggling in some areas, that's perfectly all right. Ask God to strengthen your faith. There was a time that Jesus met such a man, whose son was possessed by an evil spirit:

> *Jesus asked the boy's father, "How long has he been like this?" "From childhood," he answered. "It has often thrown him into fire or water to kill him. But if you can do anything, take pity on us and help us." "'If you can'?" said Jesus. "Everything is possible for him who believes." Immediately the boy's father exclaimed, "I do believe; help me overcome my unbelief!"* (Mark 9:21–24 NIV)

Jesus healed the boy. He did not turn him away. Another time, Jesus said:

> *The one who comes to Me I will certainly not cast out.* (John 6:37 NASU)

Jesus knows the sincerity of your heart, and He will help you!

A SIMPLE PRAYER
FOR SALVATION

Dear God,

I know that I am a sinner, and that I can do nothing to earn salvation. The best things I have done are as filthy rags in Your sight. I am sorry for my sins, and I want to live a life that is pleasing to You.

I believe that Jesus Christ is God, Your Son; that He died on the cross to pay the penalty for my sins; that He was buried; and that You raised Him from the dead as proof that You accepted His sacrifice.

I humbly call upon Your name right now, Jesus, and I ask You to save me. I accept You and what You did for me on the cross. I ask You to be my Savior. Please forgive my sins and clothe me in Your righteousness.

Thank You for saving me, for giving me the Holy Spirit, for adopting me into God's family, and for granting me eternal life.

I surrender my life to You, and I ask You to be my Lord. Lead me down the path You would have me to go. I will follow You as You enable me. Please rule and reign in my life from this day forward.

In Jesus's name I pray, amen!

What exactly happens when we are saved? Many things!

Our sins are forgiven, we are reconciled with God, and we are given eternal life—not in the future, but right now!

> *"I tell you the truth, whoever hears my word and believes him who sent me has eternal life and will not be condemned; he has crossed over from death to life."* (John 5:24 NIV)

We are given the Holy Spirit, who guarantees our eternal destiny, to live within us:

> *And you also were included in Christ when you heard the word of truth, the gospel of your salvation. Having believed, you were marked in him with a seal, the promised Holy Spirit, who is a deposit guaranteeing our inheritance until the redemption of those who are God's possession.* (Ephesians 1:13–14 NIV)

> *You surely know that your body is a temple where the Holy Spirit lives. The Spirit is in you and is a gift from God. You are no longer your own. God paid a great price for you. So use your body to honor God.* (1 Corinthians 6:19–20 CEV)

We exchange our sins for Christ's own righteousness, putting it on like a robe:

> *God made him who had no sin to be sin for us, so that in him we might become the righteousness of God.* (2 Corinthians 5:21 NIV)

> *Then he showed me Joshua the high priest standing before the angel of the Lord ... Now Joshua was standing before the angel, clothed with filthy garments. And the angel said to those who were standing before him, "Remove the filthy garments from him." And to him he said, "Behold, I have taken your iniquity away from you, and I will clothe you with pure vestments."* (Zechariah 3:1–4 ESV)

We become children of God and are accepted into His family—we are "born again" as a "new creation."

> *But to all who believed him and accepted him, he gave the right to become children of God. They are reborn—not with a physical birth resulting from human passion or plan, but a birth that comes from God.* (John 1:12–13 NLT)

> *Therefore, if anyone is in Christ, he is a new creation; the old has gone, the new has come!* (2 Corinthians 5:17 NIV)

We are actually placed "in Christ" and seated with Him in Heaven—right now! And we are placed into His body, the Church:

> *And God raised us up with Christ and seated us with him in the heavenly realms in Christ Jesus* (Ephesians 2:6 NIV)

> *Now you are the body of Christ, and each one of you is a part of it.* (1 Corinthians 12:27 NIV)

We are each given a unique spiritual gift, to benefit the Church:

A spiritual gift is given to each of us so we can help each other. To one person the Spirit gives the ability to give wise advice; to another the same Spirit gives a message of special knowledge. The same Spirit gives great faith to another, and to someone else the one Spirit gives the gift of healing. He gives one person the power to perform miracles, and another the ability to prophesy. He gives someone else the ability to discern whether a message is from the Spirit of God or from another spirit. (1 Corinthians 12:7–10 NLT)

Some of the spiritual gifts given to first-century believers are not seen as frequently today, but God knows what his Church needs and gives gifts accordingly. As God is unlimited, so is the number of potential gifts He may choose to give!

We also gain direct access through Jesus to God the Father. We ourselves are priests, and we no longer need an earthly priest to mediate between us and God. We have a great High Priest, Jesus Himself. Because we are "in Christ," when God looks at us, He sees only Christ!

Because of Christ and our faith in him, we can now come boldly and confidently into God's presence. (Ephesians 3:12 NLT)

But you are a chosen people, a royal priesthood, a holy nation, a people belonging to God, that you may declare the praises of him who called you out of darkness into his wonderful light. (1 Peter 2:9 NIV)

Since then we have a great high priest who has passed through the heavens, Jesus, the Son of God, let us hold fast our confession. For we do not have a high priest who is unable to sympathize with our weaknesses, but one who in every respect has been tempted as we are, yet without sin. (Hebrews 4:14–15 ESV)

And because of him you are in Christ Jesus, who became to us wisdom from God, righteousness and sanctification and redemption. (1 Corinthians 1:30 ESV)

That's not a complete list of what happens when we are saved, but it's a start!

Some people, especially those who are coming out of serious sins or addictions, may have a dramatic experience when they are saved. Others may not feel that anything particularly special has happened. But God does what He promises! Facts are facts, and feelings may or may not follow immediately. In particular, those who grew up going to church all their lives may not be able to pinpoint the exact time when they were saved. For each of us, the important thing is not a specific experience or event, but that right now we are believing and trusting in Jesus for our salvation!

MERCY AND GRACE

Mercy is not giving us what we do deserve. If not for God's mercy, all of us sinners would have been wiped off the face of the earth long ago, like the people of Noah's time. This would be totally just. Fortunately, God is merciful, and also patient:

> *The Lord is not slow in keeping his promise, as some understand slowness. He is patient with you, not wanting anyone to perish, but everyone to come to repentance.* (2 Peter 3:9 NIV)

Grace is giving us what we do not deserve—unmerited favor. For example:

> *Your Father who is in heaven ... causes His sun to rise on the evil and the good, and sends rain on the righteous and the unrighteous.* (Matthew 5:45 NASU)

Yet the greatest example of God's grace is what Christ did for us on the cross:

> *For you know the grace of our Lord Jesus Christ, that though he was rich, yet for your sake he became poor, so that you by his poverty might become rich.* (2 Corinthians 8:9 ESV)

God showed his great love for us by sending Christ to die for us while we were still sinners. (Romans 5:8 NLT)

He gives each of us the gracious opportunity to receive Jesus as our Savior, and to subsequently receive an inheritance with Him:

God ... has blessed us in Christ with every spiritual blessing in the heavenly places. (Ephesians 1:3 ESV)

A popular acrostic for Christians is "GRACE"—"God's Riches At Christ's Expense."

WHAT THE BIBLE SAYS
ABOUT THE HOLY SPIRIT, THE CHURCH, AND LIVING THE CHRISTIAN LIFE

After Jesus rose from the dead, why didn't He stick around on earth to build and lead His church? It was because He had something better in mind! As He said before His ascension:

> But I tell you that I am going to do what is best for you. That is why I am going away. The Holy Spirit cannot come to help you until I leave. But after I am gone, I will send the Spirit to you. (John 16:7 CEV)

While Jesus in His resurrected body could only be in one place at a time, the Holy Spirit can be everywhere at once, living in every believer, and convicting people of sin:

*And I will ask the Father, and he will give you
another Advocate, who will never leave you. He
is the Holy Spirit, who leads into all truth.* (John
14:16–17 NLT)

*The Spirit will come and show the people of this
world the truth about sin and God's justice and the
judgment. The Spirit will show them that they are
wrong about sin, because they didn't have faith in
me.* (John 16:8–9 CEV)

The Holy Spirit is God—coequal with the Father and the Son, yet
probably the least understood member of the Trinity. Perhaps the
main reason for this is that the Holy Spirit never calls attention to
Himself. He draws our attention only to Jesus:

*The Spirit doesn't speak on his own. He will tell you
only what he has heard from me, and he will let you
know what is going to happen. The Spirit will bring
glory to me by taking my message and telling it to
you.* (John 16:13–14 CEV)

*But when the Comforter is come, whom I will send
unto you from the Father, even the Spirit of truth,
which proceedeth from the Father, he shall testify
of me.* (John 15:26 KJV)

The Holy Spirit not only gave the writers of the Bible the words to
say, He actually enables *us* to understand those words!

*When we tell you these things, we do not use words
that come from human wisdom. Instead, we speak
words given to us by the Spirit, using the Spirit's
words to explain spiritual truths. But people who*

aren't spiritual can't receive these truths from God's Spirit. It all sounds foolish to them and they can't understand it, for only those who are spiritual can understand what the Spirit means. (1 Corinthians 2:13–14 NLT)

We have read that we are all born with an old sin nature. When we are saved, or born again, we are given a new nature that desires to please God and to follow His ways:

Anyone who belongs to Christ has become a new person. The old life is gone; a new life has begun! (2 Corinthians 5:17 NLT)

Let the Spirit renew your thoughts and attitudes. Put on your new nature, created to be like God— truly righteous and holy. (Ephesians 4:23–24 NLT)

Unfortunately, the old nature we were born with still hangs around, and the new nature itself lacks power. The apostle Paul described the struggles he had early in his Christian life:

I know that nothing good lives in me, that is, in my sinful nature. For I have the desire to do what is good, but I cannot carry it out. For what I do is not the good I want to do; no, the evil I do not want to do—this I keep on doing. (Romans 7:18–19 NIV)

But as Paul continues, we see that Jesus, through the power of the Holy Spirit, provides the solution:

What a wretched man I am! Who will rescue me from this body of death? Thanks be to God—through Jesus Christ our Lord! (Romans 7:24–25 NIV)

One of the most important lessons a Christian must learn is that Christ does not want us to live the Christian life by our own strength. He wants us to let Him live His life through us! We are not only to be *saved* by faith—we are to *live* by faith:

> *For in the gospel a righteousness from God is revealed, a righteousness that is by faith from first to last, just as it is written: "The righteous will live by faith."* (Romans 1:17 NIV)

> *I am able to do all things through Him who strengthens me.* (Philippians 4:13 HCSB)

> *I have been crucified with Christ; and it is no longer I who live, but Christ lives in me.* (Galatians 2:20 NASU)

> *"I am the vine; you are the branches. If a man remains in me and I in him, he will bear much fruit; apart from me you can do nothing."* (John 15:5 NIV)

> *Therefore, dear brothers and sisters, you have no obligation to do what your sinful nature urges you to do.* (Romans 8:12 NLT)

> *And because you belong to him, the power of the life-giving Spirit has freed you from the power of sin that leads to death.* (Romans 8:2 NLT)

It is the Holy Spirit that gives us this power over sin! As we allow Christ to live through us, we will not be sinless, but we will certainly sin less! And when we do sin, forgiveness is readily available:

If we confess our sins, he is faithful and just to forgive us our sins, and to cleanse us from all unrighteousness. (1 John 1:9 KJV)

But if we walk in the Light as He Himself is in the Light, we have fellowship with one another, and the blood of Jesus His Son cleanses us from all sin. (1 John 1:7 NASU)

My dear children, I write this to you so that you will not sin. But if anybody does sin, we have one who speaks to the Father in our defense—Jesus Christ, the Righteous One. (1 John 2:1 NIV)

So now there is no condemnation for those who belong to Christ Jesus. (Romans 8:1 NLT)

Becoming a mature Christian is a lifelong process. We start as babes in Christ, and we grow as we study the Bible, pray, and follow Jesus:

Like newborn babies, long for the pure milk of the word, so that by it you may grow in respect to salvation, if you have tasted the kindness of the Lord. (1 Peter 2:2–3 NASU)

As we grow, the Holy Spirit produces the "fruit of the Spirit" in our lives:

But the Holy Spirit produces this kind of fruit in our lives: love, joy, peace, patience, kindness, goodness, faithfulness, gentleness, and self-control. There is no law against these things! (Galatians 5:22–23 NLT)

Once God has begun this process in us, we are assured of its eventual completion!

> *And I am certain that God, who began the good work within you, will continue his work until it is finally finished on the day when Christ Jesus returns.* (Philippians 1:6 NLT)

> *Beloved, we are God's children now, and what we will be has not yet appeared; but we know that when he appears we shall be like him, because we shall see him as he is.* (1 John 3:2 ESV)

This spiritual growth process is one of God's purposes in the life of every believer. God wants us to be conformed to the image of His Son. But he has other purposes for us as well. We have seen that salvation is by faith, not by works. But after we are saved, God does have works for us to do, and He gives us each special gifts in order to do those works:

> *For we are God's workmanship, created in Christ Jesus to do good works, which God prepared in advance for us to do.* (Ephesians 2:10 NIV)

> *The Spirit has given each of us a special way of serving others.* (1 Corinthians 12:7 CEV)

Our purpose may be great or small—God simply wants us to be faithful to use our gifts for the task He has given us. God may want us to proclaim His good news to some remote tribe in Africa. But more likely, He may want us to raise our children peacefully and continue to work where we already work, modeling in our lifestyle His love and concern for others so that others will become interested in what makes us different from themselves. He may want us to give of our time, or of the material resources He gives us, to support some ministry. He definitely wants us to share the good news of His offer of salvation with others. And He definitely wants us to join with other believers in a local church, where we can grow, and where our gifts can help others grow:

> *Let us think of ways to motivate one another to acts of love and good works. And let us not neglect our meeting together, as some people do, but encourage one another, especially now that the day of his return is drawing near.* (Hebrews 10:24–25 NLT)

He also wants us to get His Word out to as many people as possible. The last thing Jesus said before He ascended to the Father was:

> *"You will receive power when the Holy Spirit has come upon you, and you will be my witnesses in Jerusalem and in all Judea and Samaria, and to the end of the earth."* (Acts 1:8 ESV)

We love God and want to please Him because of the love, grace, and mercy He has extended to us. But how do we know that we are His?

> *We know that we have come to know him if we obey his commands. The man who says, "I know him," but does not do what he commands is a liar, and the truth is not in him.* (1 John 2:3–4 NIV)

So what are His commands? There are not many. In fact Jesus said:

> *Come to me, all who labor and are heavy laden, and I will give you rest. Take my yoke upon you, and learn from me, for I am gentle and lowly in*

*heart, and you will find rest for your souls. For
my yoke is easy, and my burden is light.* (Matthew
11:28-30 ESV)

His "yoke is easy" and His "burden is light" because we love Him!
It is our pleasure to follow Him!

When Jesus was asked what the greatest commandment was, He
replied:

> *"'Love the Lord your God with all your heart and
> with all your soul and with all your mind.' This
> is the first and greatest commandment. And the
> second is like it: 'Love your neighbor as yourself.'
> All the Law and the Prophets hang on these two
> commandments."* (Matthew 22:37-40 NIV)

Paul expounded on this command in the Epistle to the Romans:

> *Let no debt remain outstanding, except the
> continuing debt to love one another, for he who
> loves his fellowman has fulfilled the law. The
> commandments, "Do not commit adultery," "Do
> not murder," "Do not steal," "Do not covet," and
> whatever other commandment there may be, are
> summed up in this one rule: "Love your neighbor
> as yourself." Love does no harm to its neighbor.
> Therefore love is the fulfillment of the law.* (Romans
> 13:8-10 NIV)

In particular, we are to love other believers:

> *Whoever believes that Jesus is the Christ is born of
> God, and whoever loves the Father loves the child*

born of Him. By this we know that we love the children of God, when we love God and observe His commandments. (1 John 5:1–2 NASU)

Our job is to love others, not to try to "fix" them or force them to obey God's laws. Our job is to get the Word of God and the gospel of Jesus Christ out to all people. Then the Holy Spirit can lead them to Christ and come to dwell within them. Once they are saved, the Holy Spirit will take care of whatever reform may be needed in their lives (as He does in ours).

CHURCHES, TEMPLES, AND SANCTUARIES

We usually refer to the buildings where we gather for worship as churches, temples, or sanctuaries. But these buildings are just structures made by man. It is more appropriate to refer to the group of Christians meeting in such a building as a local church.

But "the Church" is the whole body of Christ, made up of all believers everywhere, from the first century until now:

> The human body has many parts, but the many parts make up one whole body. So it is with the body of Christ. (1 Corinthians 12:12 NLT)

And the real sanctuaries or temples are the believers themselves, because God's Holy Spirit dwells within them!

> Don't you know that you yourselves are God's temple and that God's Spirit lives in you? ... God's temple is sacred, and you are that temple. (1 Corinthians 3:16–17 NIV)

> Don't you realize that your body is the temple of the Holy Spirit, who lives in you and was given to you by God? You do not belong to yourself, for God bought you with a high price. So you must honor God with your body. (1 Corinthians 6:19–20 NLT)

WHAT THE BIBLE SAYS
ABOUT SUFFERING
AND PERSECUTION

We might think that once we are saved, God will watch over us and make our life easy sailing from then on. However, that is not His way! As Pastor Charles Stanley has often said, "God is not interested in our ease, comfort, and pleasure. God is interested in conforming us to the image of His Son."

God allows suffering into our lives to build character:

> *We also rejoice in our sufferings, because we know that suffering produces perseverance; persever- ance, character; and character, hope.* (Romans 5:3–4 NIV)

Christians suffer trials and sorrows in this world (as do non-Christians) because it is a fallen world:

Here on earth you will have many trials and sorrows. But take heart, because I have overcome the world. (John 16:33 NLT)

We may also encounter suffering because of our own sins:

"The Lord disciplines those he loves, and he punishes everyone he accepts as a son. Endure hardship as discipline; God is treating you as sons. For what son is not disciplined by his father?" (Hebrews 12:6–7 NIV)

Satan will also cause trouble for us. Before we became Christians, we could not interfere with his plans. Now, we not only have the power to resist him ourselves, but we actually threaten him by seeking to lead others to Christ:

Be self-controlled and alert. Your enemy the devil prowls around like a roaring lion looking for someone to devour. Resist him, standing firm in the faith, because you know that your brothers throughout the world are undergoing the same kind of sufferings. (1 Peter 5:8–9 NIV)

If we ever doubt that God allows Christians to suffer, we have only to look at the life of the apostle Paul. He wrote major portions of the New Testament. He probably preached the gospel to more people than anyone else who lived before the age of air travel, radio, and television. Yet this is how he described his experiences:

I ... have ... been put in prison more often, been whipped times without number, and faced death again and again. Five different times the Jewish leaders gave me thirty-nine lashes. Three times I was beaten with rods. Once I was stoned. Three times I was shipwrecked. Once I spent a whole night and a day adrift at sea. I have traveled on many long journeys. I have faced danger from rivers and from robbers. I have faced danger from my own people, the Jews, as well as from the Gentiles. I have faced danger in the cities, in the deserts, and on the seas. And I have faced danger from men who claim to be believers but are not. I have worked hard and long, enduring many sleepless nights. I have been hungry and thirsty and have often gone without food. I have shivered in the cold, without enough clothing to keep me warm. (2 Corinthians 11:23–27 NLT)

As if that weren't enough, Paul also had some kind of chronic health problem, which he called his "thorn in the flesh." Most believe it was some kind of eye disease, based on various hints in his writings. As he says:

Three times I pleaded with the Lord to take it away from me. But he said to me, "My grace is sufficient for you, for my power is made perfect in weakness." Therefore I will boast all the more gladly about my weaknesses, so that Christ's power may rest on me. (2 Corinthians 12:8–9 NIV)

We may also be faced with persecution just because we are Christians. In some countries, being a Christian is actually against the law! Sometimes Christians are ostracized by families that identify with other religions. Persecution of Christians is a growing problem, even here in the United States. Still, we were told to expect it:

In fact, everyone who wants to live a godly life in Christ Jesus will be persecuted. (2 Timothy 3:12 NIV)

[Jesus speaking] *Do you think I have come to bring peace to the earth? No, I have come to divide people against each other! From now on families will be split apart, three in favor of me, and two against—or two in favor and three against.* (Luke 12:51-52 NLT)

One reason for this persecution is that Christianity is not "politically correct" as that term is understood today. We in the United States stress inclusiveness and religious freedom, and we Christians support those concepts because we welcome anyone to come to Christ and want to be allowed to worship as we choose. However, Christianity is by its very nature exclusive! The Bible teaches us that there is only *one* way to Heaven!

Jesus answered, "I am the way and the truth and the life. No one comes to the Father except through me." (John 14:6 NIV)

Salvation is found in no one else, for there is no other name under heaven given to men by which we must be saved. (Acts 4:12 NIV)

Yes, these Bible verses say that following Judaism, Islam, Buddhism, or any other religion, no matter how sincerely or devoutly, will not save a person. How can we say we love others but not tell them this? Still, in the end, each person must make his or her own decision.

Another reason we are not considered politically correct is that we believe in the Bible, which calls certain behaviors sinful that are increasingly accepted in modern society:

> Do not be deceived; neither fornicators, nor idolaters, nor adulterers, nor effeminate, nor homosexuals, nor thieves, nor the covetous, nor drunkards, nor revilers, nor swindlers, will inherit the kingdom of God. (1 Corinthians 6:9–10 NASU)

Those aren't my words; they're quoted directly from the Bible! If we believe the Bible is God's word, and we believe that God never changes, how can we turn a blind eye to these sins? We cannot, but I do want to emphasize once again that we aren't called to fix other people's behavior. We should simply love them and lead them to Christ. Then the Holy Spirit will deal with the sin in their lives. Also, we must remember that in God's eyes, one sin is as bad as any other, and all of us sin:

> For the person who keeps all of the laws except one is as guilty as a person who has broken all of God's laws. (James 2:10 NLT)

Still, Christian organizations are being labeled as "hate groups" just because we believe what God's word says!

No matter the reason for our suffering, we have a wonderful promise to console us:

> And we know that God causes all things to work together for good to those who love God, to those who are called according to His purpose. (Romans 8:28 NASU)

This verse says that even when bad things happen, God will use them to produce good in our lives! The Bible is full of examples of this, such as in the life of Joseph and the life of the apostle Paul.

> *But Joseph said to them* [his brothers], *"Don't be afraid… You intended to harm me, but God intended it for good to accomplish what is now being done, the saving of many lives."* (Genesis 50:19–20 NIV)

> *Now I* [Paul] *want you to know, brethren, that my circumstances have turned out for the greater progress of the gospel, so that my imprisonment in the cause of Christ has become well known throughout the whole praetorian guard and to everyone else, and that most of the brethren, trusting in the Lord because of my imprisonment, have far more courage to speak the word of God without fear.* (Philippians 1:12–14 NASU)

If you suffer a particular kind of pain or loss, and God helps you through it, you will be better equipped to help others going through a similar crisis. This is just one of the ways that your suffering may produce good.

Whatever happens, keep rejoicing, keep praising and thanking God, and keep praying. God will answer, and He will give you His supernatural peace!

> *So I say to you, keep asking, and it will be given to you. Keep searching, and you will find. Keep knocking, and the door will be opened to you. For everyone who asks receives, and the one who searches finds, and to the one who knocks, the door will be opened.* (Luke 11:9–10 HCSB)

The Lord is near. Don't worry about anything, but in everything, through prayer and petition with thanksgiving, let your requests be made known to God. And the peace of God, which surpasses every thought, will guard your hearts and your minds in Christ Jesus. (Philippians 4:5–7 HCSB)

"I have told you these things, so that in me you may have peace. In this world you will have trouble. But take heart! I have overcome the world." (John 16:33 NIV)

CONSEQUENCES OF SIN

When we are saved, our sins are forgiven, and we are made right with God! However, the Bible teaches that our sins still have consequences on this earth. This seems to be a general principle built into God's creation:

> *Do not be deceived, God is not mocked; for whatever a man sows, this he will also reap.* (Galatians 6:7 NASU)

Some of the greatest figures of the Bible, though forgiven, received dire consequences for their sins.

Abraham's impatience with God's delay in giving him a promised son led him to sleep with his wife's maid Hagar. The child born of that union fathered enemy nations that trouble the children of Israel to this very day! God said to Hagar:

> *"You shall name him Ishmael ... He will be a wild donkey of a man; his hand will be against everyone and everyone's hand against him, and he will live in hostility toward all his brothers."* (Genesis 16:11– 12 NIV)

Jacob twice cheated his twin brother Esau, taking both his birthright and his father's blessing. (His name means "Supplanter", because he was born grasping his brother's heel!) Later, his uncle Laban cheated him by giving him Leah instead of her sister Rachel to be his wife, after Jacob had worked for her for seven years. Laban then made Jacob work another seven years to marry Rachel as well!

King David lusted after Bathsheba and committed adultery with her. When she became pregnant, he murdered her husband, Uriah, in an attempt to cover up what he had done. He repented, but the prophet Nathan told him:

> *"Now, therefore, the sword will never depart from your house ... The Lord has taken away your sin. You are not going to die. But ... the son born to you will die."* (2 Samuel 12:10–14 NIV)

Even though we are saved, we may still suffer the consequences of our sins while on this earth!

WHAT THE BIBLE SAYS
ABOUT FREEDOM
AND FORGIVENESS

The freedom that a believer has in Christ is a major topic of the
New Testament:

> *It is for freedom that Christ has set us free.*
> (Galatians 5:1 NIV)

> *Now the Lord is the Spirit, and where the Spirit
> of the Lord is, there is freedom.* (2 Corinthians
> 3:17 ESV)

> *So if the Son sets you free, you will be free indeed.*
> (John 8:36 ESV)

But free from what? We have freedom from the law, and from
spiritual death:

For the law of the Spirit of life has set you free in Christ Jesus from the law of sin and death. (Romans 8:2 ESV)

But Christ makes the Law no longer necessary for those who become acceptable to God by faith. (Romans 10:4 CEV)

Freedom from the law does not mean we are free to sin, but that we are free to live as Christ wants us to live. We are free from the power of sin. When we do sin, forgiveness and cleansing is readily available.

Well then, should we keep on sinning so that God can show us more and more of his wonderful grace? Of course not! Since we have died to sin, how can we continue to live in it? Or have you forgotten that when we were joined with Christ Jesus in baptism, we joined him in his death? For we died and were buried with Christ by baptism. And just as Christ was raised from the dead by the glorious power of the Father, now we also may live new lives. (Romans 6:1–4 NLT)

If we confess our sins, he is faithful and just to forgive us our sins, and to cleanse us from all unrighteousness. (1 John 1:9 KJV)

We have freedom from condemnation. All our sins have all been forgiven!

There is therefore now no condemnation for those who are in Christ Jesus. (Romans 8:1 ESV)

As far as the east is from the west, so far hath he removed our transgressions from us. (Psalms 103:12 KJV)

We have freedom from the power of Satan and his demons:

Submit therefore to God. Resist the devil and he will flee from you. (James 4:7 NASU)

We can also have freedom from fear. (I have to admit this is a hard one for me!)

Even though I walk through the valley of the shadow of death, I will fear no evil, for you are with me; your rod and your staff, they comfort me. (Psalms 23:4 ESV)

So we can confidently say, "The Lord is my helper; I will not fear; what can man do to me?" (Hebrews 13:6 ESV)

There is no fear in love; but perfect love casts out fear, because fear involves punishment, and the one who fears is not perfected in love. (1 John 4:18 NASU)

Another kind of freedom is found in forgiveness. When we harbor bitterness and unforgiveness in our hearts toward someone who has wronged us, we hurt only ourselves. Writers often liken this to drinking poison and waiting for the other person to die. The Bible tells us:

Dear friends, don't try to get even. Let God take revenge. In the Scriptures the Lord says, "I am the one to take revenge and pay them back." The Scriptures also say, "If your enemies are hungry, give them something to eat. And if they are thirsty, give them something to drink ..." Don't let evil defeat you, but defeat evil with good. (Romans 12:19–21 CEV)

Be kind and compassionate to one another, forgiving each other, just as in Christ God forgave you. (Ephesians 4:32 NIV)

Whenever you stand praying, forgive, if you have anything against anyone, so that your Father who is in heaven will also forgive you your transgressions. (Mark 11:25 NASU)

Perhaps *you* are the one who has offended someone else, and that person may have bitterness toward you. The Bible tells us that resolving such conflicts is even more important than giving:

So if you are offering your gift at the altar and there remember that your brother has something against you, leave your gift there before the altar and go. First be reconciled to your brother, and then come and offer your gift. (Matthew 5:23–24 ESV)

Sometimes the most difficult person to forgive is oneself! We know all too well the things we have done in the past (or perhaps are still doing in the present) that are displeasing to God. But He has forgiven all our sins—past, present, and future—and remembers them no more:

Anyone who belongs to Christ is a new person. The past is forgotten, and everything is new. God has done it all! (2 Corinthians 5:17–18 CEV)

Then he says, "I will never again remember their sins and lawless deeds." (Hebrews 10:17 NLT)

God wants us to be sorry for our sins so that we will repent and seek cleansing, not dwell on them and keep beating ourselves up. He wants us to have Godly sorrow, not worldly sorrow:

Godly sorrow brings repentance that leads to salvation and leaves no regret, but worldly sorrow brings death. (2 Corinthians 7:10 NIV)

We can rejoice in the freedom and forgiveness we have in Christ!

FREE WILL VERSUS ELECTION

We have seen that the Bible presents as facts some things about God that are difficult to understand. We explored one in particular, the Trinity—the three-in-one nature of God. Another such concept is that of free will versus election.

The Bible makes it very clear that humans have free will and that we can choose to either accept Christ or reject Him:

> He said to them, "Go into all the world and preach the good news to all creation. Whoever believes and is baptized [by the Holy Spirit] will be saved, but whoever does not believe will be condemned." (Mark 16:15–16 NIV)

> And it shall come to pass that everyone who calls on the name of the Lord shall be saved. (Joel 2:32 ESV)

> The Spirit and the bride say, "Come!" And let him who hears say, "Come!" Whoever is thirsty, let him come; and whoever wishes, let him take the free gift of the water of life. (Revelation 22:17 NIV)

However, the Bible teaches just as clearly that God chose (or elected, or predestined) those who would be saved before the world began!

For he chose us in him before the creation of the world to be holy and blameless in his sight. In love he predestined us to be adopted as his sons through Jesus Christ, in accordance with his pleasure and will. (Ephesians 1:4–5 NIV)

But we should always give thanks to God for you, brethren beloved by the Lord, because God has chosen you from the beginning for salvation through sanctification by the Spirit and faith in the truth. (2 Thessalonians 2:13 NASU)

For those whom He foreknew, He also predestined to become conformed to the image of His Son ...; and these whom He predestined, He also called; and these whom He called, He also justified; and these whom He justified, He also glorified. (Romans 8:29–30 NASU)

Is that just another way of saying that because God is eternal, He has always known who would believe and who would not? For as David wrote:

You saw me before I was born. Every day of my life was recorded in your book. Every moment was laid out before a single day had passed. (Psalms 139:16 NLT)

It sounds like there more to it, but we won't understand it fully until Christ returns!

I once heard J. Vernon McGee give an illustration that makes this a bit more palatable. He said to imagine the doorway leading into Heaven, with a long line of believers streaming in. Above the door on the outside is a sign that says "Whosoever Will May Come!" Above the same doorway on the inside is a sign that says "Chosen before the Foundation of the World!" Somehow both statements are true!

All we can be sure of is that from our side of the doorway, we know we have been given the assignment to get the Word of God and the Gospel of Jesus Christ out to the world so that "whosoever will" can make a choice!

11

WHAT THE BIBLE SAYS
ABOUT THE FUTURE

There are prophecies throughout the Bible. We have discussed earlier prophecies about Cyrus and about Jesus. Many prophecies have already been fulfilled, but some of the most interesting prophecies of events still to come are found in the books of Daniel and Ezekiel in the Old Testament, and the book of Revelation in the New Testament. Eschatology is the term given to the study of these future events. There are many books on eschatology, and although the subject is important, it is easy to get absorbed and to neglect the study of other more immediately practical and useful teachings. (I know this from experience!)

I want to briefly focus on some particular prophecies given in Daniel and Revelation that describe the end-time period. Daniel was given this information by the angel Gabriel:

> *Seventy "sevens" are decreed for your people and your holy city to finish transgression, to put an end to sin, to atone for wickedness, to bring in everlasting righteousness, to seal up vision and*

prophecy and to anoint the most holy. Know and understand this: From the issuing of the decree to restore and rebuild Jerusalem until the Anointed One, the ruler, comes, there will be seven "sevens," and sixty-two "sevens." It will be rebuilt ..., but in times of trouble. After the sixty-two "sevens," the Anointed One will be cut off and will have nothing. The people of the ruler who will come will destroy the city and the sanctuary. The end will come like a flood: War will continue until the end, and desolations have been decreed. He will confirm a covenant with many for one "seven." In the middle of the "seven" he will put an end to sacrifice and offering. And ... he will set up an abomination that causes desolation, until the end that is decreed is poured out on him. (Daniel 9:24–27 NIV)

Although there are differences of opinion, the generally accepted interpretation of this passage is that the Israelites ("your people") would be given 490 years ("seventy 'sevens'") from the decree of Cyrus to rebuild Jerusalem, until the time when sin would be ended and everlasting righteousness would begin. It further says that after 483 years ("seven 'sevens', and sixty-two 'sevens'"), Messiah ("the Anointed One") would come but would be killed ("will be cut off and have nothing"). The Romans ("the people of the ruler who will come") would then destroy the city and the sanctuary.

Exactly 483 years after Cyrus's decree, Messiah Jesus came but was crucified. In AD 70 the Romans besieged and destroyed Jerusalem. Everything happened just as predicted. But what about the final seven years?

It is commonly understood that the current Church Age is what Jesus referred to as the "Times of the Gentiles" in the book of Matthew:

> *Jerusalem will be trampled on by the Gentiles until the times of the Gentiles are fulfilled.* (Luke 21:24 NIV)

According to the premillennial view of prophetic interpretation, when the "Times of the Gentiles" (or the Church Age) is over, the Church (both the dead and the living) will be "caught up" to join Jesus in the air and taken to Heaven. This is referred to as the rapture and is described by Paul in First Thessalonians:

> *For the Lord himself shall descend from heaven with a shout, with the voice of the archangel, and with the trump of God: and the dead in Christ shall rise first: Then we which are alive and remain shall be caught up together with them in the clouds, to meet the Lord in the air: and so shall we ever be with the Lord.* (1 Thessalonians 4:16–17 KJV)

At this time, all Christians will come before the Judgment Seat of Christ—not to determine who will enter Heaven, because that was assured when we first believed in Jesus. This judgment will determine who will receive rewards, depending upon how faithfully we used the gifts He gave us:

> *Christ is the only foundation. Whatever we build on that foundation will be tested by fire on the day of judgment. Then everyone will find out if we have used gold, silver, and precious stones, or wood, hay, and straw. We will be rewarded if our building is left standing. But if it is destroyed by the fire, we*

will lose everything. Yet we ourselves will be saved, like someone escaping from flames. (1 Corinthians 3:11–15 CEV)

Then Israel will have its last "seven" (years), a time called the Tribulation. Because the Church is gone, God ordains and supernaturally protects a remnant of believing Jews to be His witnesses during the Tribulation:

> *He called out in a loud voice to the four angels who had been given power to harm the land and the sea: "Do not harm the land or the sea or the trees until we put a seal on the foreheads of the servants of our God." Then I heard the number of those who were sealed: 144,000 from all the tribes of Israel.* (Revelation 7:2–4 NIV)

The "ruler who will come" (elsewhere called "the Antichrist") will make a covenant of peace for the seven years, but in the middle of that period, he will break the covenant and desecrate the Jewish Temple. This event ushers in the "Great Tribulation," the final three and one-half years. Jesus himself described this terrible period:

> *For then there will be a great tribulation, such as has not occurred since the beginning of the world until now, nor ever will. Unless those days had been cut short, no life would have been saved; but for the sake of the elect those days will be cut short.* (Matthew 24:21–22 NASU)

At the end of the Great Tribulation, Jesus will return with His Church to rule and reign on earth from Jerusalem for a thousand years, a period called the Millennium. When He arrives, the Jews will realize they made a terrible mistake when they rejected Jesus as their Messiah, and they will turn to Him:

> *"And I will pour out on the house of David and the inhabitants of Jerusalem a spirit of grace and supplication. They will look on me, the one they have pierced, and they will mourn for him as one mourns for an only child, and grieve bitterly for him as one grieves for a firstborn son."* (Zechariah 12:10 NIV)

The Old Testament believers will be resurrected, along with those who came to believe during the Tribulation (both living and martyred), and they will enter the Millennium along with the believing Jews. Our old friend Job knew that God would send a Redeemer, and he had faith that he would be bodily resurrected to see this wonderful day!

> *I know that my Redeemer lives, and that in the end he will stand upon the earth. And after my skin has been destroyed, yet in my flesh I will see God; I myself will see him with my own eyes—I, and not another. How my heart yearns within me!* (Job 19:25–27 NIV)

Joining them will be some of the other nations of the world, those who were kind to His witnesses and to others who came to believe during the Tribulation:

> *But when the Son of Man comes in His glory, and all the angels with Him, then He will sit on His glorious throne. All the nations will be gathered before Him; and He will separate them from one another, as the shepherd separates the sheep from*

the goats; and He will put the sheep on His right, and the goats on the left. "Then the King will say to those on His right, 'Come, you who are blessed of My Father, inherit the kingdom prepared for you from the foundation of the world' ... "Then He will also say to those on His left, 'Depart from Me, accursed ones, into the eternal fire which has been prepared for the devil and his angels.'" (Matthew 25:31–34, 41 NASU)

The Millennium is further described in Revelation Chapter 20:

And I saw an angel coming down out of heaven ... He seized the dragon, that ancient serpent, who is the devil, or Satan, and bound him for a thousand years. He threw him into the Abyss, and locked and sealed it over him, to keep him from deceiving the nations anymore until the thousand years were ended ... And I saw the souls of those who had been beheaded because of their testimony for Jesus and because of the word of God ... They came to life and reigned with Christ a thousand years ... they will be priests of God and of Christ and will reign with him for a thousand years. (Revelation 20:1–6 NIV)

After the Millennium comes another brief period of rebellion and war, then the final judgment—that of the lost souls of all time:

Remember, we will all stand before the judgment seat of God. For the Scriptures say, "'As surely as I live,'" says the Lord, "'every knee will bend to me, and every tongue will confess and give praise to God." (Romans 14:10–11 NLT)

And I saw the dead, great and small, standing before the throne, and books were opened. Then another book was opened, which is the book of life. And the dead were judged by what was written in the books, according to what they had done. And the sea gave up the dead who were in it, Death and Hades gave up the dead who were in them, and they were judged, each one of them, according to what they had done. Then Death and Hades were thrown into the lake of fire. This is the second death, the lake of fire. And if anyone's name was not found written in the book of life, he was thrown into the lake of fire. (Revelation 20:12–15 ESV)

Finally, all things are made new!

Then I saw a new heaven and a new earth, for the old heaven and the old earth had disappeared. And the sea was also gone. And I saw the holy city, the new Jerusalem, coming down from God out of heaven ... I heard a loud shout from the throne, saying, "Look, God's home is now among his people! He will live with them, and they will be his people. God himself will be with them. He will wipe every tear from their eyes, and there will be no more death or sorrow or crying or pain. All these things are gone forever." (Revelation 21:1–4 NLT)

What a glorious future believers have in Christ!

HIDDEN MEANINGS IN THOSE OLD BIBLE STORIES

In the Introduction, I mentioned some of the Bible stories many of us learned as children. Those stories are true stories about real people, but in many cases, they are also word pictures that reveal deeper truths. I want to mention just a couple of examples.

If you remember the story of Abraham and Isaac, God commanded Abraham to sacrifice his only son. By this time, Abraham had developed such a firm faith in God that He knew God was going to fulfill His promises through his son Isaac. He was prepared to obey God's command even though it would mean God would have to raise Isaac from the dead! As they were on the way to the mountain, they had this exchange:

> And Isaac said to his father Abraham, "My father!"
> And he said, "Here I am, my son." He said, "Behold,
> the fire and the wood, but where is the lamb for a
> burnt offering?" Abraham said, "God will provide
> for himself the lamb for a burnt offering, my son."
> (Genesis 22:7–8 ESV)

Later, as he raised the knife to kill his son, God stopped him, and said:

> "Do not lay your hand on the boy or do anything
> to him, for now I know that you fear God, seeing

you have not withheld your son, your only son, from me." And Abraham lifted up his eyes and looked, and behold, behind him was a ram, caught in a thicket by his horns. And Abraham went and took the ram and offered it up as a burnt offering instead of his son. (Genesis 22:12–13 ESV)

Notice that in this instance, God provided a ram, not a lamb, for the sacrifice. But later, God did sacrifice His only son, Jesus, who is the Lamb:

The next day John [the Baptist] *saw Jesus coming toward him and said, "Look, the Lamb of God, who takes away the sin of the world!* (John 1:29 NIV)

One other story I will briefly mention is the story of Joseph. Did you know that there are many parallels between the life of Joseph and the life of Jesus? Here are just a few (from J. Vernon McGee):

Joseph was hated and rejected by his brothers ... so was Jesus.
Joseph was sold by his brothers for twenty pieces of silver ...
Jesus was betrayed by Judas for thirty pieces of silver.
Joseph resisted temptation ... so did Jesus.
Joseph, though innocent, was condemned with other criminals ... so was Jesus.
Joseph was brought from prison to rule Egypt ...
Jesus was raised from the dead to rule the world.
Joseph saved the (known) world from death by famine ...
Jesus saved the world from sin and death!

READING THE BIBLE
FOR YOURSELF

In this book, I have attempted to briefly present some of the key themes of the Bible, but please know that I have barely scratched the surface. I hope that I have stimulated your interest, and I would like to give you a few tips for studying the Bible yourself.

First, choose a translation that seems the most understandable to you. Perhaps as you have read through my quotations, some of the versions I quoted made more sense to you than did others.

Next, decide on a type of Bible. Some Bibles include only the text and maybe a few maps. Some highlight the words of Jesus in red letters. So-called study Bibles contain lots of helpful explanatory and supporting information.

The book order in standard Bibles is not in time sequence. This can be confusing, because you will encounter the same historical events in multiple books, and it can be difficult to understand exactly where the events fit on a timeline. Chronological Bibles attempt to arrange the events of the Bible in the order they actually happened. I personally find the chronological versions much more enjoyable for reading. Bibles with "harmonized gospels" combine the four gospels to give a chronological depiction of Jesus's earthly life.

There are also Bibles, both standard and chronological, that are marked off in daily readings to allow you to read through the entire Bible completely in one year, taking only a few minutes each day. Some of them go through the Bible from beginning to end, whereas others skip around so that you get some variety— for example, alternating readings from the Old Testament, New Testament, Psalms, and Proverbs. (This can be helpful because some of the genealogies, rules, and regulations in the Old Testament frankly aren't very exciting reading!)

Whatever your preferences, you can find a Bible that works for you! If you're new to the Bible, start with the book of Genesis. Then read Luke (or a harmonized gospel), Acts, and Romans, then perhaps Proverbs, before tackling the rest.

When you read the Bible, make it a daily habit. Set aside a regular time and place. Begin with prayer, asking the Holy Spirit to give you understanding of what you read and to teach you what He wants you to learn.

Back in the Introduction, I wrote that the Bible has no value unless you read it. To take that a step further, reading and studying the Bible has no value either unless you let the Holy Spirit use it to lead you to the One Whom the whole Bible is about: Jesus Christ! Jesus is the subject of the entire Word of God! In fact, the Bible says that in some mysterious but very real way, Jesus and the Word of God are one and the same! In the first verse of the first chapter of his gospel, John the apostle, under the inspiration of the Holy Spirit, wrote this introduction of Jesus:

In the beginning was the Word, and the Word was with God, and the Word was God. He was with God in the beginning ... The Word became flesh and made his dwelling among us. We have seen his glory, the glory of the One and Only, who came from the Father, full of grace and truth. (John 1:1–2, 14 NIV)

May God bless you as you read and study His Word!

AFTERWORD
MY PERSONAL STORY

I'm not saying this to brag, but God gifted me with a really good brain. I was reading well before kindergarten. I skipped the first grade, and I was offered the opportunity to skip the eighth grade, but I turned it down. I was valedictorian of my grade school and high school classes. I earned a bachelor of arts in mathematics in three years, and a master of science in information and computer science a year later. I wasn't just book smart either—I had good logic and common sense. I was well respected and had a very successful career in software and systems engineering, supporting national defense and intelligence agencies both as a government employee and as a contractor. I retired in 2013 at the age of sixty, looking forward to a long and peaceful retirement with my dear wife.

But in November 2017, my bladder suddenly stopped working! I had never really had any serious health problems before. I hoped that a cause would be found so it could be fixed. I had test after test, including ultrasounds and MRIs of my spine, pelvis, and brain, but no cause was ever found. I had to start catheterizing myself six times a day to empty my bladder, after about fifteen minutes' worth of training. I had to choose from a bewildering array of catheter types and sizes with little help, other than what

I could find on the Internet. Every time I tried to catheterize, I feared I would fail and have to go to the emergency room, which did happen a couple of times. I became very depressed and anxious, and all that fear and anxiety made catheterization even more difficult.

My family doctor started me on antidepressants and antianxiety meds, but I got little relief. I really needed to see a psychiatrist, but getting a near-term appointment proved impossible. I made the first of my three hospital visits just to see one. This was followed by group therapy, which I don't want to demean, but most of the other patients there were dealing with drug or alcohol addiction, and I had a hard time relating to that.

By January 2018, my formerly smart brain had taken a really bad detour. I decided I could not live with my problems and became convinced I would be better off dead. I was tormented all day, every day with thoughts of suicide. It didn't matter to me that my dear wife and family would miss me; I simply wanted the emotional pain to stop!

I will say that I have a very healthy self-preservation instinct, and I'm not very tolerant of pain. Even though I tried to hurt myself several times, I could never go through with it, and I fought hard to live whenever I came even a little bit close to succeeding. I think that was God protecting me!

After my first suicide attempt, my psychiatrist recommended I be hospitalized and undergo electroconvulsive therapy (ECT), which was intended to bring me out of my deep depression quickly while we were finding an effective combination of medications. ECTs today aren't like what you may have seen in old movies, but each treatment does involve intravenous drugs and anesthesia, and is a somewhat traumatic experience. I spent three and a half weeks in this second hospitalization and had eight ECT treatments and multiple medication changes. When I came home, I found that my brain had gotten much worse. I had poor focus and comprehension. I couldn't do a lot of the things I enjoyed, like reading and playing around with computers and spreadsheets. I couldn't cope with finishing our tax return, which I had started just a few weeks earlier. Even my vision was messed up (probably from one of the medications). My wonderful brain, which had always been my greatest asset, wasn't working well at all!

After discovering I was even worse than before, in just a couple of days I tried to hurt myself again, and once again I found myself stuck in a hospital, this time for two weeks. Throughout these hospitalizations, I was lying through my teeth to my nurses and doctors, saying that I no longer wanted to die and was doing better. But I also didn't really want to go home and face my poorly functioning brain. I began to think I might be institutionalized forever. I thought at least if I went home, I might be more successful with my next attempt. I really didn't expect to live much longer.

After I came home from this third hospitalization, I started visiting my psychiatrist, a psychologist, and another therapist regularly, along with whatever medical doctors I needed to see— sometimes up to five or six appointments a week. In addition to trying many different medications, I had more than forty transcranial magnetic stimulation (TMS) treatments and three ketamine infusions—both experimental depression treatments. Nothing worked. (I'm not saying they don't work for anyone, only that they didn't work for me.) I was still tormented from morning till night with persistent thoughts of suicide, and sometimes I tried to follow through. I lost about forty-five pounds and spent a lot of time in bed. I was eager to get to sleep at night because at least when I was sleeping, I wasn't thinking about suicide. I was easily exhausted, even by my morning bathing and dressing routine. This went on for months.

Throughout this time, my wonderful, loving wife stood by me like a rock. I couldn't drive, so she took me everywhere I needed to go. She rarely let me out of her sight, and she put all of her usual activities on hold. She locked up my medications and gave them to me only as needed. I even had her lock up my exercise machine because I had figured out that I might be able to hurt myself with it. She made me go out for walks with her, or I would have just wasted away. I can't even begin to say how much I appreciate all that she did for me, while she silently suffered with all the pain I was causing her.

That was the physical, mental, and emotional side of my story, but now I want to talk about the spiritual side.

I believed (and still do) that I was saved when I was just a young man. I was raised by a stay-at-home mom, and both Mom and Grandma brought my sister and me to Sunday school and church every week. I became an active participant in the youth group. I recall responding to an altar call by a visiting evangelist when I was around thirteen.

Like most Christians, I had ups and downs spiritually. I can recall times when I felt a strong connection, but I was hot and cold; when things were rough, I turned to God for help, but when things were going well, I tended to take Him for granted.

Flash-forward thirty-five years or so. After a couple of failed marriages, I married again in 2000. My wife, Janet, and I melded together wonderfully. We were introduced by a mutual friend who knew both our situations. (Janet's first husband had died suddenly from a heart attack after only three and a half years of marriage.)

We attended church together. We even worked together, and enjoyed traveling together both for work and for pleasure. In late 2006, we decided to relocate from the crowds and traffic of the DC suburbs to Alabama, where the lower cost of living allowed Janet to retire early. I continued to work until May 2013. Retirement gave me more time to do things I enjoyed, including reading the Bible and Christian books. Everything was going about as well as it could, which meant I was once again in "taking God for granted" mode.

Not entirely, though. After attending Church of the Highlands for a few years, we decided it was time to start participating in small groups, so we each joined a Freedom group. My group was led by a guy I knew from work. I knew that my prayer life was not where it should be. I had formerly used a written list to guide my prayers, but I had let that fall by the wayside some years earlier. In fact, other than in church and my rote prayers before meals, I wasn't praying much at all. I knew I needed to get my prayer life back on track, so I asked for God's help.

This was a classic example of the old adage "Be careful what you pray for."

Now we're back to where we started—in November 2017, when my bladder failed!

I had become lulled into thinking that God had put a hedge around us. Because we had both suffered so much pain in the past, I thought He was going to let us cruise through retirement. I didn't handle my new "thorn in the flesh" well at all. I thought God had turned against me, and in fact I began to question whether I was even saved at all. If I was His, why was He allowing this suffering to come upon me?

I read some books that made me doubt everything I thought I knew. Some said that many people in church, especially those who grew up in church, were just there as country-club members, and really didn't have "saving faith" in Jesus Christ. But how much faith did one need in order for it to be "saving faith"? How can faith be measured? Some questioned whether some of the standard prayers like "inviting Jesus into one's heart" were adequate. Some seemed to be piling on additional requirements beyond faith for salvation.

To be fair, remember that my brain wasn't working very well at this point. If I wasn't sure I was saved, why would I even think about suicide? But I was—all day, every day. Was I being tormented by an evil spirit? It sure felt that way! Or was my brain just "off the rails"? I began to study and learn more about spiritual warfare—how to stand against the devil and his demons, and how to drive them away in Jesus's name.

Because I wasn't doing much else at the time, I put most of my available mental capacity into revisiting exactly how one was saved and how to develop a proper relationship with God. The psychiatrist who gave me my TMS treatments (and who is also a member of my church) gave Janet and me a devotional book and suggested we read it and pray together every morning. We started doing that, and we still do it today. I once again made a long prayer list, and I started going through it almost daily. I started reading the Daily Bible on our church's app every morning before I even got out of bed.

I did as thorough an inventory as I could of my entire life, looking for sins that I had never brought to God for cleansing. I knew that at salvation, all sins are forgiven—past, present, and future. But I also knew that even Christians still sin, and we need to confess those sins to maintain a proper relationship with God.

I followed the "Steps to Freedom in Christ" process outlined by Neil Anderson in his books (see the Acknowledgments). I was appalled at the list of sins I came up with! I started with all the lying I had done to my doctors and nurses, which was already bothering my conscience. I found I had bitterness and unforgiveness in my heart toward several people who had hurt me in the past. I also found that I had hurt some people and had not asked for their forgiveness or tried to make amends. I had dabbled with some "innocuous" games, organizations, and activities in my youth that perhaps weren't so innocuous after all. My list of sins was long, but worst of all, I realized how prideful I had been at times, not just being puffed up at my own knowledge and wisdom but even taking offense when my advice wasn't sought or followed. I remembered that the sin of pride was Lucifer's sin!

I also found that I had never really made a concerted effort to make Jesus the Lord of my life, except perhaps in a very superficial way. I remembered a lot of the sermons I heard in my youth were about asking Him to be my Savior, but not many were about asking Him to be my Lord. Oh sure, there was talk about surrender and giving your life to Jesus, but I don't think I ever really understood what that meant.

But the most important thing I learned, or perhaps I should say relearned, was that my salvation wasn't dependent on anything I did, but upon what Christ did for me! If it was up to me and what I did, or whether I had "enough" faith or not, I could never be certain that I measured up and met all the necessary requirements! But fortunately, it wasn't up to me—He did all the work, and all I had to do was believe and accept what He had done!

I prayed to God once again for salvation, with all the new knowledge I had gained. I didn't really care whether or not I was saved before; I simply wanted to be sure I was saved now! I asked for forgiveness and cleansing from all the sins that the Holy Spirit had brought to my remembrance. And of course, I continued to pray for healing of my mind and body.

This went on until late January 2019, some fifteen months after it all began. We had been attending church online (we call it "Church of the Couch") for most of this period, but we had resumed attending in person in November 2018. Our church has "21 Days of Prayer" at the beginning and middle of the year, and we decided to watch the prayer services from home. On one of the later days of this event, a healing service was planned where we could come for focused prayer, anointing with oil, and laying on of hands. These services were held at 6:00 a.m., so just getting up, getting ready, and getting there was going to be a huge challenge for me!

I want to pause for a moment to say a few things about healing. We Christians believe that God can and absolutely does miraculously heal people all the time. However, it is up to Him to choose whether or not to do so. He is not like a genie—we can't just throw in a few magic words, like "in Jesus's name," and *make* Him do anything! Although the apostles had gifts of healing as confirmation of their authority, it seems that few, if any, in this day and age have the spiritual gift of healing. Nevertheless, we are told in the New Testament that prayer for healing is scriptural:

> *Is anyone among you suffering? Let him pray. Is anyone cheerful? Let him sing praise. Is anyone among you sick? Let him call for the elders of the church, and let them pray over him, anointing him with oil in the name of the Lord.* (James 5:13–15 ESV)

So on Friday, January 18, 2019, at 6:00 a.m. (exactly one year after the day my second hospitalization began), that is what we did.

I had a session with my psychologist on January 22, and he told me that I might never be free of my tormenting thoughts of suicide. Not a reassuring thought! But somewhere around January 30 or 31, those thoughts abruptly stopped. Not only that, but my brain started functioning better as well. I began to enjoy life again and to do all the things I used to do that required focus and concentration. It wasn't an immediate and total recovery, but it was *very* dramatic. On February 8, I wrote an e-mail to tell my pastor that I believed I had experienced a miraculous healing. Within just a few weeks, my brain was pretty much back to normal. My depression and anxiety faded. I stopped seeing my psychologist and my therapist. My bladder problem was still there, and even though I really hated that, I was better able to accept it, and I didn't stress out about it so much anymore. With my anxiety level reduced, catheterization became easier. As a former computer programmer, my analogy was that a critical bit had been flipped in my brain—some kind of switch had been thrown!

I do have to say that my psychiatrist had just started me on a new medication, so I can't say adamantly that I was healed by a direct act of God. However, this new medication was an old anticonvulsant drug, not normally prescribed for anxiety or depression. I find it hard to believe that such a tiny, inexpensive little pill could have fixed my brain, but whether it was God or the pill, I still consider it miraculous. As my psychiatrist said, "God does the healing, and we doctors send the bill!" Since then, I have worked with my psychiatrist to get off all of my depression and anxiety medications, including that anticonvulsant, which to me is further evidence that I was in fact miraculously healed!

Because of my healing, I have been blessed to see my only son's wedding and to see my first grandchild! I have once again seen my dear wife create beautiful quilts and do all the other things she loves to do, and I have seen her wonderful smile again. Also, I have once again been able to do all the things I most enjoy.

I am still using my prayer list, but I am also learning to pray more spontaneously. I am continuing my studies of God and the Bible to learn and grow as a Christian, and I have written this book in the hope of sharing what I have learned with others.

I want to clearly say that I realize that I very badly failed my test of faith! I did not handle it well at all. Fortunately, God is faithful and always keeps His promises! Remember this promise:

> *And we know that God causes all things to work together for good to those who love God, to those who are called according to His purpose.* (Romans 8:28 NASU)

God was able to take the bad circumstances of my health problems, and my own bad responses to those circumstances, and still "work them together for good," drawing me into a closer relationship with Him and enabling me to write this book. Hopefully, many others will benefit from reading my story.

I pray that your studies of the Bible, like mine, will lead you to a real and growing relationship with the living Lord Jesus Christ!

APPENDIX

ACKNOWLEDGMENTS AND BIBLE VERSIONS QUOTED

Although I made only a few direct references or quotations other than those from the Bible, I would be remiss if I did not acknowledge a few people who have helped shaped my understanding of Christianity and the Bible. For further information, I encourage you to check out these resources.

Billy Graham

Nearly everyone has heard of Billy Graham, often called "America's Evangelist," even though he held enormously successful crusades throughout the world. He was a spiritual advisor to every US president from Harry Truman to Barack Obama. Although he passed away in early 2018, he left behind many wonderful books, sermons, and other resources. His son Franklin and grandson Will continue his ministry, the Billy Graham Evangelistic Association. Its website is www.billygraham.org.

J. Vernon McGee

J. Vernon McGee has probably influenced my understanding of the Bible more than any other person. I first listened to him on the radio when I was a young man. I remember thinking he was very old-fashioned, and I disagreed with a lot of what he had to say. It is remarkable how much wiser he got as I got older!

His vision was to communicate "the whole Word to the whole world." His radio program teaches through the entire Bible in five years, thirty minutes at a time. When he died in 1988, his program was available in thirty-five languages. Today, it is available in over one hundred languages, and it continues to be broadcast in more than 180 countries. For those who don't want to wait five years, his entire set of messages is available on an inexpensive USB memory stick and in book form. His ministry, Thru the Bible, continues, and his books and other resources are available, many by free download. The website is www.ttb.org.

Charles Stanley

Charles Stanley is senior pastor of First Baptist Church of Atlanta and founder of In Touch Ministries. You can probably find his services on your television schedule. He has many books, sermons, and study Bibles available. I have turned to his works many times as sources for help in understanding God and how He helps us handle difficult times, make hard decisions, and deal with many other issues. His ministry's website is www.intouch.org.

Chris Hodges

Chris Hodges is founder and senior pastor of Church of the Highlands, which is my church. Church of the Highlands is based in Birmingham, Alabama, but meets simultaneously at more than twenty campuses across the state, one campus in Georgia, and also online. Its services are also provided to many of the Alabama Department of Corrections Facilities. Pastor Chris started Church of the Highlands in early 2001, and it now serves more than fifty thousand people weekly. He is a leading pastoral voice in the United States and the world today. He cofounded the Association of Related Churches (ARC), a church-planting ministry; GROW, a ministry that provides coaching and resources to pastors; and Highlands College, an accredited two-year ministry training college. Pastor Chris is a gifted teacher and is the author of several books. Church of the Highlands is centered on four key steps to Christian growth:

1. Know God—find and develop a personal relationship with Jesus Christ
2. Find Freedom—connect with others, learn to live a life of faith, and be healed from your past
3. Discover Purpose—find your spiritual gifts, and a place to use them
4. Make a Difference—use your gifts to make a positive difference in the lives of others

Church of the Highlands' website has many free resources, including recordings of past sermons and a Daily Bible, available at www.churchofthehighlands.com.

If you haven't found a church home yet, or if for some reason you are unable to attend one locally, even if you're not in Alabama, you're always welcome to join us online or in person!

Neil Anderson

Neil T. Anderson is founder of Freedom in Christ Ministries (FICM) and Discipleship Counseling Ministries. He is the author of many books, including *The Bondage Breaker, Victory over the Darkness,* and *Steps to Freedom in Christ.* Many resources are available on the Freedom in Christ Ministries website at www. ficm.org.

Biblesoft, Inc.

I'd also like to thank the folks at Biblesoft for developing the One Touch PC Study Bible software. This software can display up to eight Bible translations at once with synchronized scrolling, and it provides a huge library of searchable Bibles and Christian reference works, all hosted locally on your own personal computer. One Touch made writing this book so much easier! Their website is at www.biblesoft.com.

BIBLE VERSIONS

This is a key to the Bible versions I quoted, in alphabetical order.

CEV—Contemporary English Version

ESV—English Standard Version

GNT—Good News Translation

HCSB—Holman Christian Standard Bible

KJV—King James Version

NASU—New American Standard Version (Updated)

NIV—New International Version

NLT—New Living Translation

MSG—The Message

Printed in the United States
By Bookmasters